EQUALITY BY DEFAULT

CROSSCURRENTS

ISI Books' Crosscurrents series makes available in English, usually for the first time, new translations of both classic and contemporary works by authors working within, or with crucial importance for, the conservative, religious, and humanist intellectual traditions.

Titles in series

Icarus Fallen, by Chantal Delsol, trans. by Robin Dick

Critics of the Enlightenment, ed. and trans. by Christopher O. Blum

Selected forthcoming titles

Russia in Collapse, by Aleksandr Solzhenitsyn, trans. by Olga Cooke

The Unlearned Lessons of the Twentieth Century, by Chantal Delsol, trans. by Robin Dick

Tradition, by Josef Pieper, trans. by E. Christian Kopff

EQUALITY BY DEFAULT

AN ESSAY ON
MODERNITY AS CONFINEMENT

Philippe Bénéton

TRANSLATED BY Ralph Hancock

ISI BOOKS
WILMINGTON, DELAWARE

Library of Congress Cataloging-in-Publication Data:

Bénéton, Philippe.

     Equality by default : an essay on modernity as confinement / Philippe Bénéton ; translated by Ralph Hancock.—1st ed.—Wilmington, Del. : ISI Books, c2004.

          p. ; cm

          Originally published in French as: De l'égalité par défaut. Paris : Critérion, 1997.
          Includes index.
          ISBN: 1932236325 (cloth)
                1932236333 (paper)

          1. Liberalism. 2. Political science. 3. Civilization, Modern—1950–
            I. Hancock, Ralph. II. Title.

JC574 .B46 2004   2004102729
320.51—dc22   0407

Published in the United States by:

ISI Books
Intercollegiate Studies Institute
P.O. Box 4431
Wilmington, DE 19807-0431
www.isibooks.org

Cover design by Sam Torode
Book design by Kathryn Smith

CONTENTS

EQUALITY BY DEFAULT

TRANSLATOR'S PREFACE

RALPH HANCOCK

This is a wise book. It invites comparison with another French book, the best ever written about democracy, Alexis de Tocqueville's *Democracy in America*. As Tocqueville did for his time, Philippe Bénéton provides for ours a lucid account of the deep structure, both intellectual and institutional, of threats to the human soul. At the same time, again in a way worthy of his great predecessor, the author offers a vivid, concrete portrayal of the manners, morals, sensibilities of us late moderns, of peoples who have nearly lost the capacity to articulate and thus to recognize their own humanity. His account is illustrated and adorned by literary references that will be familiar to American readers (Shakespeare, Chesterton), but also by references that might, for many of us, suggest a delightful expansion of our horizon (Corneille, Racine, Péguy).

Bénéton's vision is sobering, to say the least, darker on balance than Tocqueville's (which was already darker, more foreboding than is commonly appreciated), but somehow not a vision of despair. Tocqueville averted fruitless reaction before the leveling advance of democracy by straining to judge the new world from the standpoint of a God beyond all aristocratic prejudices, thus finding a way to accept and thereby to channel the democratic transformation of politics and society. Bénéton's situation is of course different: he addresses a world in which this democratic and individualistic transformation of life has already proceeded far beyond the point Tocqueville provided for (if not beyond what he had the power to foresee). In our time, the option of sanctioning or sanctifying this transformation in order to moderate it is no longer viable. There is no longer any alternative to exhibiting in broad daylight the hollowness of pure, formal democracy, to plainly stating the dependence of democracy on understandings of human dignity that cannot be extracted from the pure form of democracy.

Tocqueville, despite profound aristocratic misgivings he would not purge, had something of a positive if general program for the direction of democracy to offer his readers. Bénéton has only a warning. By lucid analysis of ideas coupled with astute observation of our democratic lives, he lays bare the bankruptcy and bad faith of our democratic formalism and the hollowness and self-deception of our pride in modern mastery. And yet, although this book addresses our need to hope with little or nothing that could be called programmatic, it is not a gloomy work. This is in part because its author believes that we might still hope to preserve the last threads that tie our late-modern democratic individualism to a biblical view of the transcendent dignity of each human being. In this sense, whereas Tocqueville needed to moderate the love of some and the hatred of others for democracy, Bénéton needs to remind us why it might be loveable.

Finally, though, this book is hopeful because in it we hear the authentic voice of a man whose humanity we cannot help but admire, a man whose sometimes stern judgments against late-modern ways are never divorced from a benevolent concern for his fellow human beings. If the late-modern rebellion against all limits on rights is finally driven by a hatred of our concrete humanity, as the last pages of this book suggest, then we face down this rebellion at every moment in which we recognize a love of which we are not ourselves the omnipotent authors.

I am honored to have a part in presenting this book and this author to an American audience. I thank Arek Butler for assistance with the manuscript of the translation, as well as readers and editors at ISI for many excellent suggestions, and for saving me from more than a few errors. And I acknowledge especially the assistance of the author, my friend Philippe Bénéton, who was good enough to review every page of this translation and to assist me in solving a number of problems.

AUTHOR'S PREFACE

It is just to exaggerate what is just.
— G. K. Chesterton

This is an essay on the modern world, a world that has now reached the condition of late modernity. My purpose is less to describe this world than to attempt, by climbing on the shoulders of giants of thought, to make visible what is going on in this world and what the results have been. In Western countries, which are the sole focus of this essay, modernity (in its liberal version) spread its influence gradually over two centuries; then, in the sixties, it spun out of control. This is when it crossed a threshold, opening the era of late modernity, which one might also call the era of radical-liberal modernity. Some time later, the rival formula vanished: the communist idea died along with the regime that embodied it. Deprived henceforth of its enemy, left to itself and to its own successes, late modernity is triumphant but disenchanted. But still it continues on its way. Modernity's conquests remain incomplete in two main ways: not all human beings today are yet uniquely and wholly modern; and modern principles continue to follow the same inclination and the same logic, that of radicalization. The modern world continues to "modernize." The subject of this work is this very movement that sweeps Western civilization along, or sweeps it away. Thus we can agree at the outset that every generalization is valid only in identifying a tendency—and by no means an absolute necessity somehow inscribed in history. As La Rochefoucauld wrote, "We have more strength than will, and it is often to excuse ourselves that we imagine that things are impossible."

Finally, I would like to thank some colleagues and friends who helped me in different ways: Harvey Mansfield, Tilo Schabert, Daniel Mahoney, and Ralph Hancock. To the last, I am especially grateful: his translation is remarkably faithful, and it is also a sign of our friendship.

Some of the ideas developed here have previously been sketched or set forth elsewhere—in particular in various articles of *Famille chrétienne* and in the following collections or periodicals:

"Les langages des droits de l'homme," in *Le Christianisme, ferment d'unité,* proceedings of the colloquium of the ACCE (Cracow, September 1991), Paris, éd. Universitaires, 1992, 238–48; English version: "The Languages of the Rights of Man," *First Things,* 37, November 1993, 9–12.

"Les deux versions de la démocratie libérale," in *La vérité nous rendra libres,* proceedings of the colloquium of the ACCE (Prague, September 1993), Paris, Mame, 1994, pp. 295–300; Spanish translation: "Las dos versiones de la democracia liberal," *Revista española de filosofia,* VII (13), 1995, 121–28.

"True and False Tolerance," *Crisis,* 14 (4), April 1996, 34–37.

PROLOGUE

1

The auditorium is crowded. It is the beginning of classes in the first year of law school. The students are there, a little slow to get started but determined to take notes, to underline, to darken page after page. There is no ambiance of disorder, no spirit of rebellion—these students of the new century are light-years from earlier generations. They are without political passions; they accommodate themselves to the rules of the game that are imposed on them; they are well behaved; and they are nice. By all appearances, these are peaceful times for professors.

And yet I sense a distinct sullenness in the atmosphere. The students are here under orders; they take down the words, but they are not excited by the subjects they are studying; they lend a part of themselves because they feel obligated to do so, but in their deeper selves they are absent. At the slightest digression their attention is immediately elsewhere. As soon as the students have the feeling that I am departing from the specific framework of the class and thus from what relates to the examination, I lose them, they're gone. If I should happen to interrupt the regular flow of a lecture by expressng interest in a certain book, I sense in their attitude a leaden indifference somewhat softened by indulgence for the unaccountable tastes of professors. If I emphasize the limits of our knowledge, if I risk saying "I don't know" in order to give them an example of acknowledging ignorance and suspending judgment, I see raised pens and surprised eyes. Are we supposed to write down, "the teacher does not know"? What are we supposed to write on the fateful day of the exam? There is only one thing that keeps their attention: the test. The rest is the least of their concerns.

The job of the professor, like that of the stage actor, has its blessed moments, times when a connection is made, when the lights turn on. I have known some of these moments when the atmosphere becomes intense, when speaker and listeners are on the same wavelength—in reading a great and beautiful text, for example, or when recalling great stories from the past. But here all my efforts seem pointless. Whatever I might say of the greatness of Plato, the boldness of Machiavelli, or the insightfulness of Tocqueville, however I might try to show them that the great works are great adventures, that they are written by people "who have no fear" (Orwell), the icy atmosphere of an imposed exercise remains. The students' capacity for surprise and admiration seems to be obliterated, stifled. The bow is unstrung; they seem jaded, worn out before their time. I have the feeling that nothing can touch their hearts.

This powerful inertia is especially perceptible in the early months. This is not because the students change but because the most reticent leave and because the course, a general introduction to political and constitutional questions, includes two quite distinct parts. The first part raises the fundamental questions, which are philosophical questions: the ends of politics, the problem of the best political order, the different versions of liberal democracy, and so on. I try to show them that these questions are not only course requirements, but that the great debates carried on over centuries by Aristotle, Saint Thomas, Hobbes, Locke, and all the great minds also illuminate fundamental alternatives, and thus that there is a reason to take an interest in them as human beings and as citizens. In other words, I try to involve them, to give them knowledge that matters for their lives; this does not determine their choices, of course, but it aims to put life more under the control of reason. That is the traditional mission of the university. But this is no longer commonly understood. Students do not want to invest themselves; that is not what they are there for—real life is elsewhere; why doesn't the university mind its own business?

The second part of the course, devoted to French constitutional law, is more technical. Students sometimes struggle, but they are more at ease. At bottom, they are looking for raw knowledge. They are uncomfortable with disputed questions, vital issues, avowals of ignorance. "We are already embarked on our journey in this world," Pascal said. Maybe, the students implicitly respond, but that is none of your business.

Of course I am simplifying and generalizing excessively. Among some, I think, the bow is not unstrung and the interest is real; a number of excellent papers serve as evidence and increase the professor's morale. But such exceptions do not disprove the rule: the minds and hearts of most are not open to true intellectual work.

2

Why this attitude, which has become more pronounced in recent years? Some students, a growing number, are lost in the university; unequipped or disinclined to learn, they waste a year or more. To give an extreme example, one student whom I was questioning in an oral examination on a certain book we had analyzed in class answered me quite matter-of-factly: "You know, I don't like to read." Many are worried about their future and this anxiety causes them to adopt a utilitarian attitude. But there is also something else. The spirit of the age pervades the consciousness of students and leads to this fact: for most of them, knowledge is radically cut off from life. All Western education was founded on the guiding idea that culture is a treasure of powerful thoughts and deep experiences; the analysis and discussion of great texts will serve to broaden the mind and lead it toward greater autonomy. But no idea could be more foreign to today's students. To study in order to be liberated from opinion and convention, in order to enlighten and enrich one's life, to study by attending to voices from the past—what a notion! No, true life has nothing to do with the university. On the one hand, there is education, with its required exercises; on the other, there is life, with my own personal choices. This dissociation occurs in primary and secondary school, and it goes on from there. In effect, how are we to conceive the idea of vital knowledge when autonomy is no longer a lofty goal but a given? That is the key: students, or many of them, feel and believe themselves to be autonomous. "Vital questions are beyond rational discussion; they are matters of opinion and not of knowledge, and all opinions are equal. Let each person decide for himself, and all choices are equally valid. In this case, let the professor mind his own business! When he takes up vital questions and claims to enlighten them by methodical discussion and by experiences he calls profound, he is violating my sovereign and arbitrary freedom; he is encroaching on my rights. By what right may anyone harp about what old Socrates said? He had his philosophy, and I've got mine."

From this perspective, the university no longer has anything to transmit, and the student asks nothing of it except knowledge of a utilitarian kind. Knowledge is only a tool; it has no connection with the way one lives. The feeling of autonomy anchored in the prevailing relativism of the day relaxes the desire to know and closes the mind. It follows that the relation between teacher and students tends to change. It remains unequal, to be sure, but this inequality is perceived as purely functional; it withdraws into the realm of technical competence. During class time and within the limits of a specialized discipline, the student admits without difficulty that the teacher knows more than he. He plays the game, but only provided that significant questions are excluded. As soon as they walk out the door, students are the same as their professors; they are equal and isolated by this very equality. Outside the strictly "professional" relationship, teachers and students are strangers to each other.

This state of mind has increasing influence over the university and those who teach in it. Students aspire to the knowledge of specialists, and this is how professors increasingly see themselves. The university has less and less in common with its original calling as the ideal place for the autonomous work of reason, the disinterested search for truth, and the transmission of a heritage. It becomes rather a soulless place where academic specialties coexist and proliferate in disorder. It no longer has a guiding principle. Henceforth, life has nothing to do with reason; consequently, the circle of knowledge shrinks, and it has no center. The university is emptied of substance, a victim of equality by default.

None of this benefits the students. It certainly does not contribute to their autonomy. He who challenges or is incited to challenge all forms of authority becomes vulnerable to social pressures. There is one thing that cannot fail to surprise us: how is it that these allegedly autonomous students are all so alike? Late modernity has accomplished this tour de force: it preaches autonomy and produces conformism. Our autonomous children are well-behaved children: autonomous because they are modern, autonomous within the circle traced by modern ideas. Is this autonomy not then a confinement? Is it not also a form of abandonment? Can the modern imperatives that adults, or certain adults, inculcate in generations of youth help them to live? How many youths, as victims of the sprit of the age, are fundamentally crippled by this modern-style autonomy, to which they see no alternative?

PART ONE

SCORCHED EARTH

CHAPTER 1
THE STAGES OF THE RIGHTS OF MAN

The *rights of man* is one of those majestic terms that, like *liberty* or *democracy*, has a troubled past in the public square and has been put to many uses. The rights "declared" by Jefferson or by Mounier should not be confused with those of 1793 as interpreted by the Jacobins; the Universal Declaration of 1948, framed amidst the confrontation of incompatible doctrines, was in fact universal only by convenience and pretense; the rights now proclaimed by ecologists or feminists are not of the same nature as those invoked by the Roman magisterium since Pius XII. The meaning of rights is a muddled question: though the rights of man have acquired a self-evident authority in modern societies, the nature of the "evidence" itself is unclear. To see the matter more clearly, distinctions must be introduced: there are various versions, various languages of the rights of man, at least one of which is a trap. More precisely, there are three great, overlapping stages in the history of the rights of man, which might be characterized as follows: (1) the official birth of the rights of man, or the moderate liberal version; (2) the ideological stage and the subversion of the rights of man; and (3) the radicalization and the loss of substance of the rights of man, or the extreme liberal version.

1

"Every human being as human being has rights, the same rights as every other human being. The sole fact of being human confers the fullness of the rights of man; the sole fact of being a human being trumps every distinction among men. The individual's rights are independent of birth, of condition, of wisdom, of virtue; they belong to his very humanity. From this point of view, all men are equal." Though these propositions have now lost all their revolutionary tenor, their consecration in solemn declarations at the end of the eighteenth century signified more than the end of a social order. A new world was beginning, different from preceding ones; we had crossed the threshold of the modern world. The great rupture, in other words, was the following: modern equality marked the entry into a unified world, the end of a time when birth set limits and when natural or conventional distinctions tended in varying degrees to crystallize into differences in nature. From that point onward, no human being was to be viewed as other than human; no one was inferior in his essence, there was no one whose origin, condition, or qualities reflected a difference in nature. What had been taken for granted from time immemorial—that some are by nature worthy of commanding, others destined by nature to obey—was now illegitimate. It followed that the social order must be rearranged.

Of course the idea of the primary and fundamental unity of the human race was not novel; it was an integral part of Christian teaching. But aristocratic society, officially Christian, mostly ignored the scope of these principles and tended to forget that the equality of God's children has universal implications. No doubt things are not so simple and a number of nuances and distinctions would be in order here. Still, it remains that, as a general rule, there has been a gap, if not a chasm, between the religious conviction, professed by all, of the essential similarity of all men and the feelings experienced by the Great with regard to the small. Christian equality remained, as it were, abstract, embodied little if at all in human relations. The feudal nobleman, Tocqueville writes, believed himself to be "of another nature than the serfs," and a few centuries later "Mme. de

Sévigné [could] not conceive clearly what it meant for someone who was not a gentleman to suffer."[1]

Modern equality brought down this social order and various false conventions. In the democratic social state, the human race does not recognize differences in kind; men are first of all equal. But in the name of what are they equal? What is the foundation of modern equality, of equal rights? At the end of the eighteenth century, at the time when the rights of man were consecrated in solemn texts, the answer was not obvious. Was modern equality inspired by Christianity, or was its inspiration non-Christian or even anti-Christian? Are these equal and universal rights affirmed by modern natural law an extension, a fulfillment of classical and Christian natural law, or are they instead the translation of a change of direction? The question is difficult and much debated. Besides the interweaving of influences, the main difficulty seems to be the following: the rights of man are formulated in general and equivocal terms; they are in part indeterminate—what do they mean at bottom? By emphasizing differences among competing interpretations, we may sketch the possibilities in the following way:

1. The rights of man are of Christian inspiration. The source of modern rights is found in the Christian idea of the person, which elevated man and endowed each human being with his own unique, irreplaceable value. Modern natural law represents an advance in the consciousness of the dignity of every human being; through a better understanding of natural law it corrects and extends the ancient teaching. This progress is inseparable from the ferment of the gospel.

2. The rights of man are of Christian origin but also result from a break with Christianity. Modern equality is not the translation but the secularization of Christian equality. God vanishes, but not without leaving a legacy, the idea of equality transposed by the modern world from the spiritual to the temporal realm—for better (Hegel), or for worse (Nietzsche).

3. The rights of man are born in a radical break with Christianity (and with the ancient heritage it had assimilated). According to the

Christian idea of equality, or to Christian natural law, men share a common vocation, they are governed by the same ends. In the modern version of equality, what men have in common is the right to pursue different ends, the right to have nothing in common except this right. Ancient natural law appeals to nature in order to remind man of his duties; modern natural law appeals to nature in order to loosen the reins of freedom. Modern equality is indeed new in every respect: the equality of sovereign individuals cannot be deduced from the natural law of ancients and Christians; it is no longer the equality of the children of God. The modern idea of emancipation marks a clear break with the past.

How then shall we find our way? The issues are unclear and seem to resist any simple solution. These modern principles were developed within a world shaped by Christianity, but their elaboration is inseparable from a reaction against the political power of religion, and, in the first instance, against the Roman church. They became authoritative in an ambiguous context, the outcome of a century in which Christianity had buckled under the assault of the Enlightenment but had by no means surrendered. The members of the French Constituent Assembly did not at all agree on the meaning of the various articles of the Declaration of 1789 or on the implications of the reference to a Supreme Being. Likewise, if the God invoked by Jefferson in the Declaration of Independence was perhaps little more for him than a rhetorical formula, the same cannot be said for all the Founding Fathers.

Thus, there is no unity of tone, but there does seem to be a dominant theme—that of a break with the past, albeit a theme partially muted because it is not pursued to the fullest extent. What are the implications of the dominant version of rights, that is, liberal modernity? It associates the principle of equality with two rejections and thus two emancipatory formulae: the casting of religion outside politics, and the rejection of the *bona vita* as the end of political action. Classical Christian politics strove to promote rules of life; modern politics (liberal version) limits itself to setting the rules of the game. For natural law as it is understood from Aristotle to Saint Thomas, man is drawn toward a vocation and the end of politics is the fulfillment of this vocation. Politics is in the service of the good way of life, the *bona vita multitudinis*. In this perspective, the language of classical Christian natural law emphasizes above all the duties of man.

Modern thought, on the other hand, is characterized by the rejection of the good life as the end of political action. Since men are deprived of a natural vocation, or at least cannot agree on what that vocation is, it is necessary to rethink politics with a view to men as they are and to enable men to live peaceably together even though they do not agree on how to live. The work of modern political thought, initiated by Machiavelli and then by Hobbes, and further developed by Locke, issues in a liberal or procedural solution: the duties of man give way to his rights, and the rules of life give way to the rules of the game designed to allow men, divided amongst themselves, to pursue each his own way, his own interest. The rights of man are a key component of the modern promise (in its liberal version) that contains the following elements: a promise of emancipation through individual liberty; a promise of reciprocal recognition through equality before the law; and a promise of well-being through civil peace, the mastery of nature, and the free pursuit by each of his own self-interest. In other words, the promise of a society where equally free men, recognizing each other as equals, will be able to live peacefully and to pursue individually their own private happiness (and first of all their comfort).

In its day, this liberal solution remained a moderate solution. The break was not total; it was not thought through to its conclusion. For Locke or for the French liberals or the American Founding Fathers, it was indeed a question of founding the new political order on the rights of the individual to pursue his own interest; however, they took it for granted that these principles had to be limited in their range by the moderating influence of the family, education, and religion. The *bona vita* is excluded from politics, but there remain rules that govern ways of life, rules that define what is honorable and dishonorable. Equal liberty plays out only within limits, limits inherited from Christian morality. But the Founders failed to see that they were setting a time bomb. To begin with the autonomous individual and his rights is to open up a dynamic process, that of the sovereignty of the individual, in which the rights of man break every bond with nature. It is to open the way to what was to come, to the results we see today. Whereas Christian thought said, "Here are your duties, and may God help you," contemporary thought declares, "Here are your rights, and to hell with you."[2]

2

In between Christian and contemporary thought, one might say, arise dramatic periods in which the rights of man are denatured and in which this denaturing provides good reason to transgress and profane them. Michel Villey has held the rights of man responsible for the acts of violence and terror that many have committed in their name, notably in the French Revolution.[3] But the rights of man deserve neither this much credit nor this much indignation; they were not pushed to the extreme, nor even perverted, but rather completely subverted by ideology.

In June of 1793, the day after their victory over the Girondists, the Montagnards drafted a new Declaration of Rights in which they reaffirmed individual liberties and emphasized resistance to oppression—this at the very moment they were involving themselves further in a politics of force and violence. Still, it would be a mistake to find here a contradiction between words and deeds; there is not at all a contradiction, because the meaning of the rights of man within Jacobin discourse had changed.

From the beginning of the Revolution, the activists (or "patriots") never ceased to speak in two interwoven vocabularies, one universalist and the other ideological: (1) "All men are free and equal by right"; (2) "Men are divided into two categories: the good and the evil; the first are the people, the second are the enemies of the people." The ideological vocabulary divided the world in Manichean terms in the name of the Happy City that was to be built, and thus subverted the universalist vocabulary. The rights of man lost all universal value; they were embodied in the camp of the "revolution," the "people," and "freedom." "Freedom for the people," yes, but "the people means us, and no freedom for the enemies of the people." "We are brothers," of course, but "be my brother or I will kill you" (according to Chamfort's ironic formula). Robespierre's famous phrase in which "the despotism of freedom" opposes "tyranny" would have been a contradiction in terms if, from his point of view, freedom had not been definitively embodied in a particular camp—which in effect gave "freedom" a perfect freedom to oppress. Likewise *tyranny, barbarism, fanaticism, humanity, patriotism,* etc., no longer referred to situations, acts, or feelings; rather, they were identified with the actors themselves. In Nantes, Carrier acted out of "humanity" against "monsters." Ideology says: politics is war, an inexpiable war between the good camp and the bad camp, between "two opposite spirits," as Robespierre said, the benevolent and the malevolent. This Manichean dualism subverted the rights of man.

Whereas the Jacobin revolution used two vocabularies (universalist and ideological), the Bolshevik used only one (and criticized the abstract universalism of the French declarations). Thus the Soviet experience revealed clearly what was partially concealed in the French Revolution, the logic of ideology at work. For Lenin, the war between the good and the evil exhausted reality, and therefore all had to be subordinated to this irremediable struggle. Freedom? asked Lenin—whose freedom? The freedom of the oppressors or of the oppressed? Whose rights are you talking about—the rights of the bourgeoisie to exploit the proletariat or those of the proletariat to liberate itself? Freedom, equality, justice, truth were transformed, denatured by the only point of view that counts, that of class. Ideology crushed universal values and led to this: my enemy (whoever is not with me) has no rights.

There is not, then, an ideological version of the rights of man, Jacobin or Bolshevik, that would be the counterpart to the liberal version. There is, instead, a liberal version of the rights of man and an ideological subversion of these rights. The two paths of modern politics are not at all symmetrical.

This ideological experience has practically come to an end with the 1989–91 fall of the Soviet regime. Ideological hope has collapsed. Universalist principles have won, and the rights of man embody the spirit of our times; their logic continues to unfold. Considered as an ideological revolution, "the French Revolution is over"; as a liberal revolution, it is picking up speed.

3

Just what happened in the West apart from the dramatic episodes of ideological domination? One might, from a certain distance, respond as follows: on the one hand, liberal modernity has made tremendous progress in the promised direction; on the other, the logic of modern principles has been unleashed—the time bomb has exploded—and the rights of man have been at once radicalized and emptied of their substance.

In many respects liberalism has kept its promise: people have won equal recognition before the law, individual liberty, civil peace, and comfort. Social life in itself no longer offends human dignity; life in community has become more secure, and life itself sweeter. The liberal formula has forced the mighty to contain their pride; it has restrained the powerful and inaugurated an era in which no one is any longer surprised by the profusion of material goods. If one looks at things not in the short term but from a historical perspective, what a success! The political success is particularly undeniable and remarkable: in the West, politics still divides men, but political disagreements are handled peacefully and no one risks life or liberty by displeasing those in power. The rights of man have played and continue to play a protective role, and the Minotaur (political power) has been domesticated. This success is even more evident in the material realm: scientific and economic progress have allowed the great majority to reach that level of material well-being that Saint Thomas said was a condition of virtue. This progress has also lengthened life, reduced pain, provided much free time and much entertainment. Equality before the law, security, liberty, and the "comforts of life"—the liberal project seems to have succeeded beyond all hopes.

Yet, from another point of view, the dynamic of modern principles has gone much further than Locke, Montesquieu, or Madison could have expected. The rights of man sprung up in soil prepared by Christianity; and even if these authors distanced themselves from Christian doctrine, they did not tear up all its roots. These roots held fast for a long time, but the storm of the sixties swept away all before it and thus ushered in a new period, that of late modernity. The idea of the sovereignty of the individual shook off all limits, and the principle of equality and equal liberty took on a radical form. In Corneille's *Le Cid*, Rodrigue once said to Chimène: "J'ai fait ce que j'ai dû, je fais ce que je dois." ("I've done what I must; I shall do what I must.") Now, late-modern man says: "I do what I want, and no one's better than me," or, more precisely, "Each individual is sovereign, and each is the equal of any other; I live how I like and my way of life is as good as anyone's." Modern emancipation now appears identical with pure or indeterminate freedom.

The effect of this evolution has been to empty the universalism of the rights of man of all substance. Men are the same but they no longer have anything in common but this pure and indeterminate equal freedom. Man as sovereign no longer has an end specific to his nature; his rights are not defined by his human nature; instead, his very rights define him as human. The universalism of the rights of man is reduced to mere procedures, and thus these rights are without foundation. For how can the rights of man be grounded rationally if man is reduced to his rights? How can one invoke the source of human dignity if there is no criterion by which to distinguish worthy from unworthy conduct?

Rights are detached from nature and thus without any anchor. They multiply and proliferate in a chaotic profusion. As originally understood, the rights of man were based on a distinction: on one hand, the realm of rights where humanity as such received its due, where no distinction between men applied; on the other, the rest of life, in which differences among men were played out. But this distinction is effaced along with the idea of nature. If rights are no longer based on nature, then there is no reason to limit them. Anything one wants can become the object of a right.

> It appears possible to reformulate, without violence or artifice, all natural desires, as well as all the commandments of the law, in the vocabulary of the rights of man, or, as is said in English, human rights. If man has a right to life, he also has a right to death, or at least to a death with dignity; if he has a right to work, he has a right to leisure; if he has a right to live in a country, he also has a right to travel; if a woman has a right to a child, she also has a right to abortion; if she has a right to respect, she also has a right to pleasure, even to orgasm. In brief—since we should stop here—there is nothing under the sun or moon that may not become the occasion for and the object of a human right.[4]

As objects of rights proliferate, so do the subjects claiming these rights, and for the same reason: emptied of all human substance, human rights are detached from man as man. Rights become particular; they no longer belong to humanity as such but only to certain people. This is a general tendency, but it is particularly strong in the United States, where the rights of groups and groups seeking rights have multiplied: rights of blacks, of women, of children, of the poor, of Native Americans, of homosexuals, of the homeless, of victims, of the overweight, of nonsmokers. . . . As the categorical language of rights pervades social policy, what happens to the very idea of the rights of man?

Rights have been carried further still; they have crossed the threshold of the nonhuman. Radical environmental movements have taken up the cause of animal rights. Man is but an animal among others, he is dehumanized. But since every right implies a corresponding obligation, it remains to convince cats of the rights of mice, lions of those of gazelles, and leeches of the rights of man.

At the provisional end of this history, rights no longer have any precise meaning and confusion reigns. Nature, invoked at the beginning against convention, has itself become a mere convention. The logic, or *one* logic, of modern equality has done its work in at once inflating and ruining the rights of man. The modern world has lost its way, the victim of a particular version of equality: equality by default.

CHAPTER 2
THE TWO VERSIONS OF EQUALITY

From the beginning, therefore, modern equality is equivocal or composite. On the one hand, it reflects the recognition of the dignity of each human being as such; on the other, it involves a potential subjectivism that leads to the severing of equality from nature. This potential has been realized: the equality dear to late modernity has broken entirely with everything associated with the premodern world, and first of all with Christianity; it is not at all a *substantial equality*; it is a purely formal equality, or an *equality by default*. These two versions of equality are at opposite poles from one another. The first is grounded in the recognition of what is human, the second in the refusal to consider any act to be specifically human. According to substantial equality, the other is my equal because we share something that distinguishes us as human beings; according to equality by default, the other is my equal because he cannot be more "human," that is to say better, than me. In the first case, men are equal because such is the truth of human nature; in the second, men are equal because human nature is a fiction. On the one hand, men are alike before they are different; on the other, they are alike because they are free to be different, and no difference is worth more than another: they are alike because they are different. Modern thought, which proclaims the rights of man, has come down to this: these rights have no justification but by default—they are not justified by man's being but by his lack of being. Every man benefits from an equal freedom; each one does what he wants with his life, because to live humanly no longer has any meaning.

1

What is the basis of substantial equality? At first sight, human beings are unequal in a number of ways: they are stronger or weaker, bigger or smaller, more or less gifted in a footrace, in eloquence, at the piano, in mathematics; they have varying degrees of will, charm, courage, and so on. Substantial equality is based not on a negation of these inequalities but on something beyond them. Beyond all these natural inequalities, there is a primary and fundamental equality.

Such is the supernatural equality of Christian teaching, the equality of the children of God. Human beings are equal because they are of the same family (all beloved children of God the Father, and therefore all brothers), because they are all heirs of the same history of love and infidelity (Creation, Fall, Redemption), because they all share the same condition (sin) and the same destiny (supernatural). All are of the same high birth, all injured by original sin, all redeemed and "worthy of God's blood" (Bernanos), all called to participate in divine felicity. The God of Christianity is a person who willed each human being as an individual, who created each one as a unique person, irreducible to any other, armed with free will and the freedom either to respond or not to respond to his calling. The great adventure embraces all of humanity and each individual human being. No one is left out, be he powerful or wretched—"God accepteth no man's person" (Galatians 2:6). The outcome depends on the heart of each individual human being; each one holds his salvation in his hands. Christian universalism applies first of all to a spiritual realm.

Yet this equality of the children of God does not exclude distinctions or inequalities that will be consecrated on Judgment Day: every human being will be judged according to what he has done with what he has received (the parable of the talents). Such an inequality, inaccessible to human knowledge, is beyond all human conventions and beyond all differences of social condition; it even goes against the grain of these differences insofar as they give rise to a haughty and proud spirit among the Great. What is specific to Christianity and a "scandal for the Jews, folly for the Greeks," is the condescension and humiliation of God become man to the point of being nailed on a stake of infamy. The incarnation bound indissolubly *sublimitas* and *humilitas*, and the words of the gospels confirmed what Nietzsche would later call "the transvaluation of all ancient values": greatness is in humility and self-effacement; it is in the renunciation of greatness. "If any man desire to be first, the same shall be last of all, and servant of all" (Mark 9:35). This reversal provokes the rage of Nietzsche, who sees in it "a rebellion of everything that crawls against that which has elevation" (*The Antichrist*). How is it possible to aspire to the status of the overman without rejecting, vomiting this God of the Christians, who through the incarnation abdicates all greatness and majesty,

> A god who, loving us with an infinite love,
> Was willing to die for us ignominiously

as Corneille's Polyeucte said? The paradox of Christian inequality is that it teams up with Christian equality to undermine human pretensions.[1]

Substantial equality can in another sense be understood as a natural equality, grounded in the universality of human nature and of the human condition. Human beings are part of one and the same humanity; they are alike prior to being different. From this viewpoint, substantial equality is a matter of natural law, either secondarily (in the Christian version) or fundamentally (in the secular ver-

17

sion). In what way are human beings naturally equal? They are equal because "every man bears the whole form of the human condition" (Montaigne), because from the moment a human being knows himself to be a human being he cannot fail to recognize his likeness in another. In other words, men are equal because what they have in common takes precedence: all are born of a man and a woman; life is given to them; they have not chosen it any more than they have chosen their family, their language, their country, their historical period; they are all equally passing through this life, equally lost in the immensity of time and space. All things pass, life is brief, man falters with age, his final hour is unavoidable and uncertain, this world is mysterious and absurd. Everyone needs others—man is born dependent—and all (with extremely rare exceptions) live in society. All are made of the same stuff and subject to the same constraints and passions, those evoked eloquently by Shylock in *The Merchant of Venice* in order to plead that a Jew is made like a Christian:

> I am a Jew. Hath not a Jew eyes? hath not a Jew hands, organs, dimensions, senses, affections, passions? fed with the same food, hurt with the same weapons, subject to the same diseases, healed by the same means, warmed and cooled by the same winter and summer as a Christian is?—if you prick us do we not bleed? if you tickle us do we not laugh? if you poison us do we not die? and if you wrong us shall we not revenge?—if we are like you in the rest, we will resemble you in that. If a Jew wrong a Christian, what is his humility?[2]

Men are equal in their limits and their infirmities, and also in what gives them a unique status in the universe (at least until some new dispensation). Man is an exception in nature and, unlike the other animals, he is not reducible to his biology. All human beings are endowed with reason; and, though they are minuscule in the universe, they are the only ones who know this, while the universe knows nothing of it. No one has spoken better than Pascal of this misery and grandeur that all human beings share.

But if all men participate in the same humanity, why have they not always known this? Our awareness of the nature common to all human beings has progressed through history, at least up until the time of equality by default; it has overcome the foreignness of the other and sharpened the natural feeling of human identity. Nevertheless, this awareness remains ever vulnerable to the barriers erected by passions and false ideas, and which led in the extreme case to the murderous folly of the Nazi regime. Still, once reason has broken through such blinding obstacles and prejudices, human beings, at critical times, naturally recognize their common humanity. Our sense of otherness looks ridiculous when looked at from afar, and no less so at the side of a human being who is suffering or dying, or one who is lifted up in great joy. In life's great experiences, especially great trials, man recognizes his likeness in the other; he feels that our simple humanity comes first. G. K. Chesterton said this in his own way:

> We should say, after a somewhat disturbing discovery, "There is a dead man under the sofa." We should not be likely to say, "There is a dead man of considerable personal refinement under the sofa." We should say, "A woman has fallen into the water." We should not say, "A highly educated woman has fallen into the water." Nobody would say, "There are the remains of a clear thinker in your back garden." Nobody would say, "Unless you hurry and stop him a man with a very fine ear for music will have jumped off that cliff." . . . [A]ll of us have [this emotion] in connection with such things as birth and death. . . .[3]

The great books, which bring to view the most vital experiences, make the same case. It is because they strike chords that belong to man's very humanity that they transcend their time and are always alive. When Job cries to heaven, when Priam comes to implore Achilles, when Hamlet hesitates, when Andromache sacrifices herself, we see ourselves in them despite differences between us; the unity of nature speaks to us and we meet them across the centuries. This meeting is inseparable from the feeling of human dignity. Human beings do not commune with each other in abjection. Substantial equality is intrinsically tied to an awareness that, in Samuel Pufendorf's words, "the very word man carries with it the idea of dignity."[4]

On the other hand, this primary equality of nature and of condition does not erase natural inequalities. Human beings are first of all equal in that they belong to the same family, but they are unequal in various activities and most profoundly in the order of being. All Western humanism springs from a fundamental idea that may be expressed as follows: man is a divided and hierarchical being, an animal distinguished by his reason, a "reasonable animal" who must govern himself by following what is most elevated in him. His dignity resides in his reason—not, of course, in his mere cold and calculating reason, but in that integrating reason that is nourished by all the human faculties. The human being worthy of this name governs his freedom by his reason, entrusting it with the task of checking his passions, as represented by Plato's charioteer who controls his two steeds, black and white. But from this point of view men are quite unequal; they follow reason and honor human dignity in varying degrees. In the extreme, some radically betray their calling as human beings, as when, functionaries of horror or slaves of their passions, they degrade another or themselves or both: when the SS-Führer or the Commissar treats his fellows as beneath humanity, when the gangster orders foul murders, when the sadist abandons himself to his desires, when the drug user sinks into addiction. . . . Not every act of man is a human act.

Thus human beings are at once equal and unequal; they are first of all and fundamentally equal, and secondarily but significantly unequal. The great difficulty consists in holding these two facts together—a primary and essential equality on the one hand, and a considerable range of difference on the other. The deeper one goes, the more human beings appear at once equal and unequal. But equality always takes precedence.

2

Equality by default is of a completely different nature; it is founded on an idea of humanity that breaks totally with Western humanism. It is a radical equality that excludes all vital inequality. Man is pure indeterminacy, equality without compass, freedom without vocation; man is what he makes himself. Nature is no longer opposed to convention; it is itself no more than a mere convention, the last from which one must be weaned. Consequently, no hierarchy remains in the structure of human being or among the various ways of being. Reason abandons its governance over the passions, it loosens freedom's reins. The rupture is complete: reason is cut off from life; it no longer has anything to say about ways of life. The vital questions are matters of opinion, and all opinions are equal. Default man is liberated from every norm and every model; he no longer forms part of an order that transcends him. He enjoys a sovereign independence. He is a stranger in the universe.

Equality has thus been emptied of all substance: when thought of as equal autonomy and carried to the extreme, it is necessarily an equality by default. If human beings are equal by virtue of a substantial commonality, this equality is mixed to varying degrees with inequality, this substance is shared to varying degrees by each person; being is thus characterized by degrees, by hierarchy. In order for men to be equally and radically autonomous, they must have nothing in common but the freedom to have nothing in common. It follows that man's essence resides entirely in a freedom reduced to the freedom of indifference, an arbitrary choice, dissociated from reason. There are no longer worthy and unworthy acts. If anything remains of human worth it lies entirely in the free act itself.

What remains, then, of differences among human beings? Unlike substantial equality, which combines equality with the recognition of differences, equality by default implies the elimination of differences, and in particular the rejection of all vital distinctions, distinctions that bear on ways of being. Whatever one's way of life, everyone is like everyone else.

The vocabulary of "respect for differences," of "tolerance," does not address the problem at all, since it belongs fully to the world of equality by default. In other words, "the right to be different" is subsumed under the rule of likeness. How does this conversion work? The meaning of the formula in effect breaks down into two propositions: (1) The right to be different applies only to certain differences; (2) These differences make no difference.

On the one hand, equality by default attacks all differences that threaten the equal autonomy of individuals, that is, all differences based on natural attachments and all those that appeal to a natural hierarchy of acts and of works. It tends to blur any difference between men and women, children and adults, young and old, or (in the case of environmental extremists) human beings and animals. Its effect is to eliminate all distinction between reason and unreason, decency and indecency, the sacred and the profane, genius and farce, master and disciple, profound and superficial experience. The models of excellence that have characterized Western civilization—the wise man, the hero, the saint—are no longer distinct from their contraries. The world is homogeneous. Here, the "right to be different" does not apply.

On the other hand, certain differences are accepted, proclaimed, extolled—namely, those differences in terms of which the radical autonomy of the individual, his limitless liberty, his rejection of traditional moral norms are affirmed. The "right to be different" means primarily the right to live with whom I want and how I want, the right to change "partners" (as in bridge) when I want, the right to dress eccentrically if I want, in all circumstances. An American television network broadcast some time ago a story about a man who lived with nine wives. The tone of the commentary expressed no surprise—that is to be expected—and at the end a neighbor stated the moral of the story with a big smile: *"That is America."* He did not mean, "How healthy we are here!" but rather, "Here in America, everyone lives as he likes and yet this does not make anyone different." Thus he expressed perfectly the meaning of "the right to be different": human beings no longer distinguish themselves by their ways of life. There is no difference between nine wives and only one, no difference between a couple of the same sex and a union between a man and a woman, between a makeshift family and a stable family in which the children issue from the same parents. If people are considered to be different and free to be different, this is only in order to affirm that this makes no difference. The "right to be different" implies the equal freedom to live as one pleases and the prohibition of any moral judgment on ways of life; it means the denial of all moral difference grounded in nature. In other words: whatever I do, no one is better than me. All choices are equal and beyond discussion. Universalism by default undermines all moral universalism: the question of living well, of the *bona vita,* has lost all significance: to each his own "values"; the Self rules and sets the standards of its own good. So why did Madame de Clèves, Madame de Tourvel, Madame de Renal struggle within themselves? Why were Lady Macbeth, Lord Jim, Raskolnikov riven by remorse? Why did Phèdre condemn herself? Why does Horace reproach Camille? Why does Rodrigue hesitate? Why does Hamlet search his soul? So much for these tales: *anything goes.*

Under the reign of equality by default, every rule of life is banished, every dogma is outlawed with a single exception—that of relativism. Whoever claims to escape this rule infringes on the freedom of another and presents himself as a superior person. But by what right? In the name of what principle? What can such a person be up to? Who does he take himself to be? The sphere of legitimate ideas shrinks under the pressure of this "moral" imperative: the denial of vital distinctions. In the kingdom of equality by default, individuals are kings—as long as they submit to the rules of individualist subjectivism. Beyond good and evil, it is evil to speak of good.

3

The antiracist campaign launched in France in 1985 with the slogan *"touche pas à mon pote"* ("don't mess with my man") achieved great popularity. Organized by certain young people apparently working in complete independence from "established" antiracist organizations and political parties, a few false notes hardly detracted from its impact. It benefited from the goodwill of the mass media, from the blessing of government agencies, and by all appearances from widespread support. But what is the meaning of this slogan?

"Touche pas à mon pote" does not mean the same thing as "we are all brothers." The formula is more than imperative; it deliberately scorns all respect for forms. It is decidedly casual concerning proper usage (dropping the "ne," employing slang), and familiar, to say the least (the style, the familiar verb form), in its manner of address. It posits a relation of equality in definite and charged terms, terms that express a certain aggressiveness and convey a leveling intent. According to Chesterton, there are two languages of equality. One says, "You are as good as the Duke of Buckingham"; the other, "The Duke of Buckingham is no better than you." The first draws one upward; it is the vocabulary of substantial equality. The second pulls downward; it is that of equality by default. *"Touche pas à mon pote"* obviously belongs to the vocabulary of equality by default; the slogan extolls equality not through the elevation of some, but rather through the debasement of others: the Duke of Buckingham is no better than "my man." The formula demands equality but not mutual respect. Substantial equality confers honor on human beings; equality by default is an equality without honor. In the first case, human relations are respectful of forms that convey consideration for another; in the other, they deliberately ignore forms and

thus become more blunt, more rude, more brutal. "Sir, I am honored," one might say in the former case; "hey, man!" in the latter.[5]

To pass from one form of equality to the other is to witness a change in the nature of human relations. Upon reflection, the fundamental difference is seen to be the following: substantial equality implies the recognition of the other; equality by default requires only a recognition without substance, a recognition by default: what I recognize in the other is no more than a full and complete independence, the independence that I first claim for myself. Consider the relation between persons of higher and lower status. (Social inequalities persist even in the world of equality.) Under the rule of substantial equality, each recognizes the other as kin: "The differences between us do not affect what we share fundamentally and what accords us both the full and complete dignity that follows from being human." By contrast, where equality by default operates, a person only recognizes in another that which makes him a stranger: "No one lives more worthily than I, not you nor anyone else, because the notion of worth has no meaning. Live as you like, and so will I. There is nothing vital I can receive from anyone. Goodbye"—so speaks the person of a lower status. "I grant you that; my way of life is no better than yours. I am stronger than you but we are equally free. You live as you please; I'll live as I please. I have nothing more to say to you. So long"—so answers the person of higher status. Substantial equality brings men together; equality by default separates them.

Let us recapitulate. The two versions of equality imply two very different interpretations of "we are alike": On one hand, "we share the dignity of being human"; on the other, "you are no better than me." On one hand, "we are alike despite our differences"; on the other, "we are alike because our differences are meaningless." One says, "my fellow human beings are my neighbors"; the other says, "my fellow human beings are strangers to me." The modern world is not what Hegel thought, the world of reciprocal recognition; it is instead that of the affirmation of self, and of mutual indifference.

But one must go further still. When a person is enclosed in his Self and thus cut off from others, he suffers from not being recognized by his fellows. As a consequence, each Self must seek this recognition, which runs precisely contrary to the rule of the Self. The Self is indifferent to the other as other, but it needs the other to see itself in the regard of the other. What becomes then of the world? Is it not a "masked ball," as Stendhal might have said? We shall return to this theme: is not modern man, who wants to be self-sufficient, alienated by this very desire?[6]

CHAPTER 3
THE ALMA MATER AND THE NECKTIE

Wherever equality by default reigns, the individual tends to take priority over the institution (family, school, state, etc.) and the latter tends to be reduced to a loose assortment of functions and procedures. Duties thus tend to fade and with them their associated forms. In the university, one sign of such a fading is unmistakable: collars are opening.

1

Since May 1968 law professors have rarely worn the traditional robe, except for thesis defenses and in the more traditional disciplines. As a general rule, the tie has replaced the bands of ermine trim, but exceptions to this rule are increasing with the passage of years and the succession of generations. Thus there are now two kinds of professors: those who wear a tie, and those with an open collar. I belong to the first group; it would not occur to me to teach a class or to attend a faculty committee meeting without a tie, not to mention more casual dress. To do so would make me feel that I was slipping, cheating on the obligations of my profession, debasing the institution. And yet I am not particularly attached to this strangely shaped piece of material that has to be tied around the neck. So why give in to what is after all nothing but a convention? By habit or conservatism, perhaps, but also because of what this convention signifies. This piece of material is much more than just that; it has a symbolic dimension and is full of meaning.

What is the main difference that separates the two kinds of professors? Of course the difference is not absolute. It holds only as a tendency, a disposition, an inclination. But the tendency is clear: the professor who wears a tie indicates by this sign that he considers himself a professor, that he adheres to the traditional role of the professor. The tieless professor indicates that he does not consider himself a professor (on the traditional model); by the absence of this ornament he declares his distance from the traditional role; he redefines his professional role. To button or not button one's collar—this question therefore matters: from one gesture to the other the conception of the profession changes in nature. Equality by default is at work here.

Let us take a closer look at this phenomenon. In the name of what would one wear a tie to teach a class? From a practical point of view, teaching requires no particular outfit—it's about talking. One can talk just as well in sandals or in shoes, in a kilt or in pants, wearing a tie or with an open collar. In terms of utility, what is the difference one way or another? So just what is the purpose of a necktie? Shouldn't everyone dress as he or she likes? To define a norm is to limit everyone's autonomy, to infringe upon equality by default.

The utilitarian point of view is blind to the language of forms, and the spirit of modern equality is allergic to it. Yet if clothing means nothing, why not come to class dirty and ragged? The language of forms expresses the link between dress and attitude. To wear a tie in certain circumstances is to apply the criteria that articulate the hierarchical character of life, to give effect to distinctions among activities, times, ways of being. In a world not yet overlaid by equality by default, one does not dress in the same way for a ceremony as for a picnic, to go to class or to go to a soccer game. The professor who wears a tie is refusing to consider everything as equivalent; by choosing to "dress up" in order to teach, he is saying that this activity is worth a certain seriousness and formality; he is upholding the honor of the profession and of the institution. Appropriate dress is a sign of respect for the university. It means that this grand old woman, this alma mater responsible for transmitting our past, is worthy of consideration and that her mission remains or should remain a great and distinctive one—all the more so since society is subject to the influence of equality by default. The necktie is among those symbolic forms which say to students: "Here we are serious about serious things, things that are by nature different from what you might do elsewhere."

What things? The tasks of the tie-wearing professor are not limited to the transmission of knowledge; he is also a teacher of attitudes of the intellect. Respect for forms of dress goes along with respect for forms that make up the *habitus* required for intellectual life: one does not talk the same way in jeans or when wearing a tie, and casual language is not an intellectual virtue.[1] Negligence in dress and grooming is likely to carry over into the life of the mind. The professor teaches much more than the content of his lectures. It matters what he says, but also who he is. The following are some of the habits of mind that a professor must develop in his students: to proceed in an orderly fashion; to make progress step by step; to fix the mind on its object; to avoid lazy approximations; to admit one's ignorance; to submit to what is real—in sum, to achieve knowledge rigorously, to cultivate reason, and avoid sloppiness. I think for example of an admirable professor, Raymond Aron, and of that "famous voice of bronze . . . to which so many students listened without a moment's lapse of attention, and who learned from this voice self-mastery, mistrust of passions, rigor, and 'simple and tranquil' honesty."[2] Respect for forms is a component of this education of the mind and spirit. The necktie possesses an educative virtue.

2

Still, many of our colleagues no longer share this view. In France and elsewhere, though lawyers and medical doctors still commonly wear ties, they are becoming rare among sociologists, psychologists, educators, and rarer still among mathematicians, physicists, and chemists. Philosophers, historians, and literary scholars are divided: logicians, for example, wear the open collar whereas moral philosophers wear ties; history and literature professors are more inclined to open their collars the more they tend to adopt the new methods in the human sciences. Why these differences between disciplines and subdisciplines—differences that, one might add, extend to the kinds of ties worn? But let us leave aside nuances and exceptions. The key, roughly, to an explanation seems to be this: those who remain faithful to a humanist conception of knowledge wear ties; those who believe in pure, hard science do not. What is in question here is not people's devotion to their work, but rather how that work is understood.

The scientistic professor is in tune with equality by default. For him, reason is impotent to rank activities, attitudes, or works. Thus teaching must be neutral whenever the question of a way of being arises. In other words, teaching is severed from education defined as the shaping of our humanity. The scientistic professor has no properly educative role to play, no example to give; he is there to deliver a body of knowledge, cold and neutral, to teach techniques and methods. Thus he is free to distance himself from the traditional role. By not wearing a tie he manifests his autonomy in the area of ways of being just as he recognizes the same autonomy in his students. The professor may play at not playing the role of a professor; his role is limited to the teaching of a specialty, a function like any other. The relationship of roles between professor and students is narrowed; it is freed from the traditional ways of the university and limited to obeying the formal rules of the institution. As a professor, the scientist hunkers down in the sphere defined by his technical field and a certain set of rules—why, for example, would he go beyond his area of competence in order to verify spelling or require a stylistic correction, much less to feel obligated to provide an example through his dress and grooming? This would be paternalism. Outside the area of impersonal knowledge, of technical competence, everyone does as he pleases, the professor as much as the students.

The necktie thus appears as a "significant variable," as scientists might say. The tie-wearing professor believes in intellectual virtues; the tieless professor believes in methods; the first is concerned with manners and customs, the second holds to rules; the first is faithful to forms, the other limits himself to procedures. In the world of equality by default, virtues, customs, and forms recede in favor of methods, rules, and procedures.

Of course I exaggerate; I am forcing things a bit. I attach too much importance to ties. Doubtless it happens or has happened that an outward conformity to the traditional role is accompanied by a relaxed attitude to the obligations of the profession. Perhaps, too, in wearing a tie, I am putting on airs. Yet it remains that this piece of material has great symbolic significance and that the decline of the tie goes along with a gradual transformation of the profession and of human relations. Academic courtesy is the loser. One still finds very learned and well-behaved people at professional meetings, whose company is both enriching and charming, but more and more one meets the legions of experts, collars open, but in closed battle formation for science. Technicians of knowledge cannot be bothered with respect for forms.

3

If there is anything foreign to students, it is certainly the symbolism of forms. That is partly because of their age, but it is also because of the spirit of the times. Overall, despite differences among institutions, the rule is casual dress for girls and boys alike. This dress is more or less universal; it is appropriate to all occasions, whether going to a movie or a party, to the café, or to an exam. Where dress is concerned, students no longer distinguish among their various activities.

Why this mixture of styles? To stretch the point again just a bit, the key is this: for students, the choice of dress is solely their own business; it is an expression of the Self, indifferent to context. Ways of dress relate to ways of life, and ways of life are autonomous. Why would the nature of the activity matter since clothing concerns only the wearer? Students sometimes present themselves in sloppy dress at an oral examination; their ingenuousness is often disarming. The notion that dress might express a relationship to others and to the institution is light years from anything that might enter their heads—everyone is free, you know! More generally, the attitude of these students toward professors tends to resemble that of American students; it is characterized by a peaceful and likeable informality. Students are in no way aggressive; they are at ease and friendly and seem ready to treat their professors as just slightly older pals. What is the difference after all? A difference of technical competence, but otherwise professors and students are equally autonomous, complete, and free.

How then might one establish norms of behavior in areas where it would clearly be in the students' interest to follow them? The temptation is to let things go. Consider a student at an oral examination. He greets you with a sonorous "hello," lays some indistinct article of clothing that resembles a combat fatigue left over from two successive wars on the back of the chair, and sits down without further ceremony. In the course of the exam, I notice that he is seated askew, slumped in his chair, and I hear recitations of "yeah, yeah." Shall I say something to him? If I say nothing, I do him no service, I fail to do my job; he will be handicapped later by not knowing how to present himself. But if I say something to him, I am sure to infringe, in his eyes, on his business, to adopt the pose of an "old-fashioned" professor. Finally I decide to tell him as gently as possible to sit up straight and to articulate his "yesses." I will not have to repeat it—students are very obliging in oral exams—but I see the surprise in his eyes. In the world of equality by default, education is dying.

CHAPTER 4
SOULLESS INSTITUTIONS

What is happening in universities illustrates a more general phenomenon: institutions are losing their soul. Appearances are maintained, but social roles are emptied of substance. Equality by default does not put an end to hierarchical relations; it changes their nature. These ideas are not new; they were developed a century and a half ago by Tocqueville in an analysis one cannot but admire. What is the meaning of this "equality of conditions" in which Tocqueville sees the characteristic trait of modern or "democratic" society as opposed to earlier "aristocratic" societies? It means first of all that equality is inscribed in the law and that concrete equality is progressing. But it also means, more profoundly, something else: what characterizes modern society is not so much the disappearance of social inequalities—there are still leaders and the led, superiors and inferiors—but rather that these inequalities take on a new significance.

1

One of the most illuminating passages of *Democracy in America* is that in which Tocqueville analyzes "how democracy modifies the relations between servant and master."[1] These few pages are a model of perspicacity and insight. In Western societies, both old and new, Tocqueville explains, one finds masters and servants; on this point, there is no distinction between the democratic and the aristocratic social state—apparently nothing has changed. And yet everything has changed: the relationship between master and servant has been transformed; however unequal in its essence, this relation cannot escape the gravitational force of modern equality. The power of Tocqueville's analysis lies in his ability to pierce through appearances and to see what lies in the realm of feelings and ideas.

Just how, then, has this relationship changed? Among aristocratic peoples, servants constitute, on the basis of their personal subjection, a separate people governed by a fixed order; their way of living transposes the aristocratic spirit of the masters to their own servile condition. In the democratic social state, on the other hand, "equality of conditions makes the servant and master new beings and establishes new relations between them." Servants are no longer attached to their condition, they no longer constitute a distinct society. The master is not by nature superior to the one who serves him; he only becomes so by contract, for a determinate time and function. "Within the limits of this contract one is servant and the other master; beyond these limits, they are two citizens, two human beings. . . . In democracies, servants are not only equal among themselves; one can say that they are in a way equal to their masters." The master would no more dream of guiding or helping the servant than the servant would take the master for a model. The function fulfilled or the contract completed, the relationship comes to an end, and the servant becomes the equal of his master and a stranger to his household. Tocqueville does not go so far as to say that this sense of equality will finally abolish the master-servant relationship, but his analysis points in this direction. A century was sufficient for the near disappearance of domestic servitude in modern societies.[2]

Let there be no mistake about the meaning of this analysis. Tocqueville welcomes the disappearance of the false convention on which aristocratic society is based (that birth distinguishes human beings), but he is worried about the disappearance of the sense of obligation that was associated with superior ranks. Inequalities take on a narrower, more technical meaning; they become purely contractual and functional; they no longer embody anything that engages the heart and creates indissoluble bonds. Hierarchy becomes naked and cold. Has this analysis ever been truer than today? It is valid, as we have seen, for the university, as it is also for schools, for the family, for churches, and for the state.

Take the example of today's school. It seems to function as it always has: students, teachers, classes, homework, grades, recreational activities, and so forth. To be sure, some changes are readily visible: classes are coed, students no longer form rows, there is no more giving out of prizes, casual dress is the rule (on both sides), technological equipment is the source of the principal's pride, and so on. School has been "modernized," but it is still school: teachers teach, students study—what more could one ask? And yet there has been a profound change; the spirit is no longer the same. The relationship between teachers and pupils is miles away from what Péguy describes in *L'Argent* [Money] or Pagnol in his remembrances of childhood. The break came in the 1960s: equality by default was at work, and it has had its effect within the schools.

Consider a teacher of mathematics affected by the new spirit. He wears jeans, his speech is relaxed—but no matter, he is a math teacher, and the rest is no concern of his. A pupil comes to class with his hands black with grease. Will the teacher send him to wash his hands? It's not his business, and anyway the pupil would not take the suggestion kindly. Now take a teacher of the old school: he sees one of his pupils in the street. He is barely twelve years old, and he is smoking a cigarette. He allows himself to remark: "You're a little young to smoke." The pupil, surprised, even offended, opens wide his eyes. His attitude says: "But what business is that of yours? At school, I learn your lessons, I do your exercises. Beyond that, keep your advice to yourself. Do I concern myself with your life?"

Or take a class studying French in which the teacher subscribes to the modern pedagogy. He no longer considers himself a teacher of literature, charged with providing a knowledge of substance, with shaping minds and tastes, with transmitting an inheritance. He sees himself as a technician of language and a facilitator in the service of free expression. The nature of teaching is thus transformed; it becomes emptied of content and aimed at the acquisition of skills. Why give priority to classic literature when Pascal is no better and no worse than any other author, when his style of writing is just one technique among others? Knowledge is only a toolbox; beyond technique all opinions are equal and free, and one has only to see that they are expressed. So our teacher gives priority to newspaper articles and "social problems"; concerning these he teaches formal rules and solicits opinions from students where substance is concerned. Classes tend to be filled with flimsy and chaotic chatter. If a student defends theft, the teacher raises no objection; if the discussion veers towards obscenity, he shows no surprise. Let each say what he has to say. Tolerance is the rule. "Dupont, explain this verse of Racine," said the teacher of old. "Xavier, give your opinion on the media," says the modern teacher.

Consider finally a philosophy teacher faithful to the tradition. He reports: "The difficulty I most often face in my classes is that I cannot teach the systems of Plato, Descartes, Hegel, or any great philosopher without one of my students saying: 'That is what he thinks; I think otherwise. I respect his opinion, so you respect mine.'"[3]

Both form and content have changed in the schools. The teacher considers himself or is considered by others less and less an educated person and more and more someone who is "trained," a technician of knowledge; thus he relieves himself, or is relieved by others, of any broader educative mission. The formation of taste, of character, of will, of civic spirit is no longer within his competence. How can a school educate when it refuses to distinguish between an educated and an uneducated person? How can it shape a human being when it no longer knows what a human being is?

In the family, the same causes produce the same effects: relations between parents and children are gradually emptied of substance and education disintegrates. Consider modern parents. They have one or two children, they watch over their health and check on their school grades, but otherwise they let things go. In a way, these are the terms of a contract that is subject to endless bargaining. "I want a motor scooter," the child says. "That depends on your grades," his mother answers. "I want to go on vacation with my pals," says the adolescent. "All right, but first pass your exam," replies his father. Modern parents do not impose anything; they negotiate and renegotiate in order to obtain the desired result within their narrow domain of competence. The relationship between parents and children is more and more restricted and specialized; it tends to become purely functional. Parents have no rules of life to transmit; they do no allow themselves to say "you must"; they give life but are careful not to give instructions for its use—to do so would be to deny the child's freedom, to violate his rights, to prejudice his choices. The child learns about life from his own world: music, friends, radio, television. "She is living her own life," the father says. Besides, if he intervened, it would be resented as an intrusion.

Parents involve themselves less, and they feel less involved. Children, who are becoming rarer, are increasingly considered as a passing moment in the lives of parents. This is particularly noticeable in the United States, where the child is treated like a guest passing through, a guest to whom one owes certain courtesies but who will before long fly off on his own wings. The thought of separation is already a separation. The family is no longer a community woven together with indissoluble bonds; it is rather a contractual and contingent association, a collection of autonomous individuals. Each member of the family must freely achieve fulfillment, the child as much as the parents, but the child is not to be in the way of his parents' fulfillment. Wherever equality by default reigns, all are equally free: children are no longer children, and parents are no longer parents. (Of course this account is too stark, but the tendency it describes is real.)

This decline of authority has many other facets. Churches have lost many of their members, and members feel more autonomous vis-à-vis their church. This is particularly true of the Catholic Church and its moral teaching: the Roman magisterium affirms the inviolability of objective moral laws, whereas many Catholics, especially in the United States, dissent on this point and adhere to the modern norm, which recognizes no authority but individual conscience. Nor has politics been spared; it is increasingly limited to establishing the rules of the game and managing interests. The substance of life escapes its competence, and the sense of a common destiny tends to disappear—the indeterminate rights of the individual fill the whole political landscape. The political leader is no longer someone chosen by his fellow citizens for his political talents and virtues and entrusted with the high responsibility of the common interest; he has become a mere delegate for the administration of public matters. As a result, political discourse takes on a new twist: men in power and their competitors for the most part adopt a vocabulary of expertise. In politics and just about everywhere else, responsibilities are giving way to functions. What is a head of state? A man like any other who performs the function of a head of state. A judge? A man like any other who performs the function of a judge. A priest? An ordinary man who performs the function of a priest. A mother? A woman like so many others who performs the function of a mother. At the heart of the modern world, established inequalities change in nature because their object is shrinking, because this object is increasingly confined to the realm of technical competence and no longer involves, or involves less and less, a way of life. Modern man is autonomous. Ends (which impose themselves on us) give way to objectives (which depend upon our will). Hierarchies of competence remain, but there are no more authorities.

2

There are no more authorities. By this we mean: equality by default tends to suppress or to undermine institutions that, as institutions, had traditionally been invested with a certain intellectual and moral responsibility, with a vital responsibility—institutions such as, above all, the church, the family, schools, universities, and the state. Modern man welcomes this: "How long will you treat men like minors? Your authorities are nothing but individuals like any others; how do you expect to impose their arbitrary judgments on others? Authority is dead—let's dance on its grave!" But to speak in this way is to forget that some of the human beings in question are in fact minors (children), and it is to ignore or wish to ignore what an established authority is in truth. The decline of authority has two sides: on the one hand it means the refusal to recognize authority because such recognition restricts individual autonomy; on the other hand, it means the refusal to exercise authority because such exercise also violates individual autonomy.

Authority comes with a certain responsibility, which is associated with certain forms. Now, a responsibility is no more a function than a form is a procedure. In both cases, the difference is the same: a responsibility or a form has to do with ways of being; it has a vital significance, it is a matter of substance. The person who exercises a function hires himself—or, rather, a part of himself—out; he has no other responsibility than that of an agent in a system. The person who takes on a responsibility invests himself, he assumes a burden that obliges him as a human being. To fulfill a responsibility is to belong to an institution (not an organization), to put oneself in the service of a moral (or religious) idea, to embody a mission. The schoolteachers of whom Péguy speaks with such moving gratitude fulfilled a responsibility because they put themselves in the service of something greater than themselves. They owed their authority to what they embodied, what they strove to embody: the school and its educative mission. When a teacher initiated his students with the words "here, gentlemen, one does not lie," the children felt that this was not an individual who expressed a preference but the teacher who spoke—one who was in the service of a great institution, who did not do whatever occurred to him, but who did what he was supposed to do.

In the same way, the job of the statesman, judge, officer, doctor, or mother confers authority only insofar as it is exercised as a responsibility, only when the individual disappears behind what he or she embodies—the common interest, justice, military service—when he gives himself to what is to be done. Authority is not in the service of the one who exercises it; it is itself a form of service.

Of course human beings do not always measure up to what they are supposed to embody. But responsibilities support and uphold individual persons, thanks in particular to the forms attached to these responsibilities. Forms, unlike procedures, have a meaningful content; they have a symbolic dimension. Provided they are alive and authentic, that they have not fallen into a soulless formalism, they are crutches that help people hold themselves upright and fulfill their obligations. They represent the dignity of responsibilities, the duties inherent in them, the respect due to them, and they indicate that authority is not an attribute of a person, but that it has to do with what the person represents, with what he must serve. "The soldier," Jeanne Hersch explains,

> must salute the officer, even if the officer is drunk. He does not salute the drunk man; he salutes the symbol embodied by this man, a symbol of the army and of the hierarchical order that made him an officer. The officer, for his part, must be convinced that it is not himself who is being saluted. If he derives arrogance or power from the salute, he immediately destroys the symbol. The one who must respect authority the most is the holder of authority; he must feel humble before the symbol he embodies. Authority should be a school of humility and not a source of arrogance. . . . Nor is the teacher this teacher in particular, with his defects and good qualities. It is impossible that all teachers should be sublime, but they are all teachers. It is not their excellence that is recognized in class; it is rather the fact that they embody the calling of the teacher. It is this sym-

bolic situation of the teacher that constitutes his authority. . . . I would say the same thing concerning the authority of fathers and mothers. Why must the father be respected? It is not for his exceptional qualities; it is because he is the only father his children have.[4]

The better we understand what is symbolic and alive in forms, the more solid institutions will be, and the better they will support those who accept the responsibilities attached to them.

Modern man winces at this. How can he consent to such a responsibility when he sees himself above all as autonomous? Modern man does not abandon himself; he does not give himself to a mission that transcends him. He holds onto what is his. If he occupies a position of traditional responsibility, he is careful to keep his distance: the modern professor no longer dresses as a professor, the modern principal addresses his young colleagues familiarly, the modern clergyman or officer dresses like a civilian as soon as he has the chance, the modern mother asks her children to call her "Monica" or "Theresa" rather than "Mom." By transgressing traditional forms, modern man affirms his individuality; he affirms his autonomy vis-à-vis an institution. All in all, he looks to extricate himself, and thus to be free of all vital responsibility. The father who plays the pal or technical advisor to his son relieves himself of the moral burden of fatherhood; the professor who has only technical knowledge to transmit is dispensed from providing an example or from the burden of eliciting respect; the judge who considers himself a legal technician is not required to uphold the honor of the law, and so on. Functional inequality has only functional obligations; it knows nothing of duties pertaining to one's status, of noblesse oblige. Equality by default also liberates the man on top.

But is the man on the bottom as liberated as he thinks? Though authority may give way, influence is felt more than ever, in particular in the discourse of those who claim technical competence or who present themselves as the interpreters of public opinion (experts and journalists), and in the biased representation of reality provided by the Information and Entertainment Machine (the media). The society ruled by modern equality is not a society without elites but a society in which elites recognize no traditional or moral responsibilities.

3

In the world of equality by default, people are both equal and unequal in a peculiar way: they are equal in their lack of being, and unequal in their having. Only having—functional competence, money, external success—distinguishes human beings. In this world, the weak are left without resources. To treat a child as an adult is to abandon him; to tell a helpless young man to do as he likes is to have done with him; to treat an old man with juvenile informality is to humiliate him; to tell a subordinate whose life is spinning out of control, "that's your problem," is to fail him; not to give up one's seat to a pregnant or aged woman is to fall short of what we owe to others. Equality by default cannot establish just relations between the strong and the weak—power knows no duty.[5] The world of equality by default is cold. As Tocqueville saw, societies in which the spirit of modernity is at work atomize so that only associations based on common interests remain. Equality by default undoes social bonds; it distances human beings from each other.

4

Let me be clear about something. There is a time for everything—a time to speak in favor of institutions, of responsibilities, of forms, and a time to speak against them. Today is a time to make the case for institutions, because they are under siege; in an earlier day, many criticisms were welcomed because institutions could be suffocating. Institutions are corrupted when two principles wane: the spirit of service, and scrupulous respect for individual persons (and every person is unique). Thus French middle schools of old produced many rebels when they were characterized by abuse of authority and arid formalism. Here is the testimony of the philosopher Alain,[6] who was never able to forget "the odor of the refectory."

If you are not familiar with it, you are lucky. That proves that you were never confined within a certain kind of school. That proves that you were not a prisoner of order and an enemy of the law from your earliest years. Since then, you have shown yourself to be a good citizen, taxpayer, husband, and father; you have learned little by little to undergo the influence of social forces; you have recognized a friend even in the state police officer, for family life taught you to make a pleasure of necessity. But those who have known the odor of the refectory will never be brought to order. They spent their childhood pulling at the rope that bound them—which, finally, one day, they broke. And so they entered life like suspect dogs, dragging a piece of rope. They will always get their back up, even when offered the most appetizing food. The will never love anything having to do with order and rules; they will always be too afraid to respect these. You will always see them enraged against laws and regulations, against refinement, against morality, against the classics, against pedagogy and against academic honors, because of all the smells of the refectory. And this olfactory condition will undergo an annual crisis, just at the time of year when the sky goes from blue to gray, and when the bookstores display classic books and school bags.

Alain's brilliant remarks make the case for procedures, which protect against abuses of authority. Nevertheless, procedures will never be sufficient—except to make soulless families, lifeless schools, and states without substance. In every case one must find an equilibrium point that cannot be determined a priori. Everything depends on the state of manners and morals; there is no pure solution.

CHAPTER 5
KNOWLEDGE AS ACCOMPLICE

Modern man benefits, one might say, from a great privilege: where vital questions are concerned, he has nothing to learn. It is not that he is endowed with innate knowledge; it is just that there is nothing to be known about life's great questions. The Socratic question—how should a man live?—has no object; there are as many answers as there are individual choices. In other words, opinions occupy or tend to occupy the whole ground, and knowledge is driven into retreat. Modern equality is incompatible with all vital knowledge; it works to transform our understanding of humanity.

In this enterprise, the modern mind has a privileged adversary and a weighty ally: its adversary is one form of knowledge, and its accomplice another. The adversarial knowledge, the one that must be disqualified as a form of knowledge, is culture; the ally or accomplice is not science itself but the scientistic version of science, in particular as it is applied to human things. Between culture (philosophical and literary) and equality by default there is a radical antagonism: culture is aristocratic by nature; it sets apart certain men who are greater than us, works that go further in the exploration of reality than we could go by ourselves; it holds that the company of great minds enriches being, that it opens the way to a more profound and autonomous life—but each of these claims is an affront to the equal autonomy of every individual posited as an immediate datum of existence.

On the other hand, equality by default and pure, hard science are on the same wavelength; they collaborate to disqualify culture and being. The scientistic version of knowledge gives equality by default the support of "science," and it finds a natural home in the world of modern equality.

1

The scientism that accords with modern equality derives from what one might call the second version of scientism. The nineteenth-century version has effectively had its day: it claimed to disqualify, once and for all, religion, philosophy, and tradition and to replace all these prescientific forms of thought with rational knowledge. Scientific reason lit the path of Progress; it was destined to govern life. The science of our times no longer has these ambitions; it has retreated to its own domain and declares itself a stranger to the question of "values." But strengthened by its extraordinary successes and its universal prestige, it has not backed down on its claim to be the only authentic form of knowledge. Whatever lies outside the scientific method lies outside reason.[1]

Science *stricto sensu*, that is, mathematics and the natural sciences, intimidates and sometimes fascinates the other disciplines. It has no need of others; it leads its own life, which bears no relation to the common experience of mortals or to the knowledge characteristic of other disciplines. The break dates from the seventeenth century, when science cut itself off from philosophy and the perceptible world. Nature is written in mathematical terms, Galileo exclaimed, and the Galilean revolution has cast the scientist into a separate world. The nature studied today by the physicist or the chemist is made up of atoms, molecules, cells; it is foreign to the nature that offers itself to one who lives in it. It is odorless and tasteless, neither welcoming nor threatening; it has nothing to say to the human senses. And yet scientists feel pain as much as anyone else; they can appreciate, or at least so one hopes, the quality of a wine or the beauty of a landscape. But as soon as they don their smocks, nature loses every attribute other than its mathematical properties and becomes a homogeneous world from which all quality disappears. This world of science is also a separate world because it is in a way suspended in air. Science cannot give an account of its object of study. Why does the universe exist? What accounts for this being, that event, this history, which escape all general laws? Nor can it explain or justify itself: why the intelligibility of the universe and thus the possibility of science? Why dedicate oneself to science rather than cocaine trafficking? There is no scientific answer to these questions.

Modern science is without a doubt a great venture illuminated by the brilliance of great thinkers, and scientific knowledge has made tremendous progress. But this progress concerns only one region of the real. Scientism closes science upon itself, taking it to be the only form of reasoning that counts; in this way it tends to discredit vital questions, which are relegated to the nonscientific darkness. Moreover, as Husserl pointed out, it undermines the meaning of nature as natural world. The scientist in the thrall of scientism (though not of course the scientist as such) is similar to the "learned personage" mocked by Mephistopheles (*Faust,* pt. 2, act 1):

> What you do not touch is for you a hundred leagues away;
> What you do not grasp for you does not exist;
> What you do not count seems to you untrue;
> What you do not weigh for you has no weight;
> What you do not convert to cash for you has no value.

This closing of reason has wreaked still worse havoc in the domain of properly human questions: the old "moral and political sciences" have given way to modern "human sciences" in which the scientistic inspiration is dominant. The "human and social sciences" (dominant version) have put themselves under the tutelage of the "exact" sciences and have thus rallied under the banner of method. They have proclaimed their autonomy with respect to philosophy and have adopted the point of view that seems to promise the only worthwhile form of knowledge, the scientific point of view. In Aristotle, the object comes first, and since the objects of knowledge are by nature different, they imply different modes of knowing. For scientists, the object, that is reality, must surrender its arms; method rules, and what is knowable is knowable only through one sole way of knowing. Scientific reason is confused with reason, period.

The result is that the hardcore human sciences burn bridges. Throughout history, philosophers and writers have conversed and argued, but even when they have argued, they have been speaking to one another. They are part of the same family. The human sciences, for their part, are not of this family; they have nothing to do with this heritage. All dialogue becomes pointless because the new sciences dismiss with a wave of the hand the questions the Western tradition held to be central—the existence of God, the essence of humanity, the good life—and they recognize only those answers that pass through the filter of method. The great works thus lose their status as great works. It is no longer a question of understanding great thinkers as they understood themselves in order to better understand the world; it is only a matter, on occasion, of explaining them, science providing the means to take the creator's place in articulating the meaning of his creation. Culture is no longer a living tradition and an opening to the world; it is a dead collection of objects of the sciences like so many other objects. Method implies a blank slate. In its radical version, the human sciences treat a lack of cultural learning as a virtue and a program. They attack culture, since they intend to replace it.

All this calls for a number of qualifications. What is in question is of course not sociology, economics, psychology, and the like, as such; what is in question is the scientistic version of the human sciences, now the dominant version in the United States, in France, and elsewhere. Of course, on closer inspection things are more complicated and more nuanced: there are indeed gradations between radical scientism and the rejection of scientism—for example, between pure, hard sociology and that which is inspired by Tocqueville. There is considerable disorder in the human sciences (fragmented as they are among disciplines and subdisciplines); there are also differences between countries, times, areas of research, and so on. But the general tendency is clear: scientism as applied to the human sciences advances irregularly, but it always advances, and always in the same direction. The decisive moment, once again, took place in the 1960s, when the scientistic version of the human sciences swelled up in every sense of the term, taking over many important professional positions and playing the role of counselor to the prince: social problems would not resist scientific solutions. The setbacks of social policies inspired by social scientists have no doubt tarnished their prestige, but the human sciences still continue to gain ground gradually in schools, in universities, and in society at large at the expense of culture, especially of literary studies. The reason for this is simple: equality by default clears the path for human sciences and pushes in the same direction. How can one resist the sirens of the spirit of the age? Militant scientists are doubt-less less numerous than those who have more or less been taken in by dominant ideas. Today scientism finds an ally in conformism.

What is the basis of this complicity between scientific knowledge concerning man and equality by default? It lies in three ideas prop-agated by scientism, ideas that harmonize perfectly with modern equality: knowledge is cut off from being; reason is cut off from life; stripped of being, the other collapses into the same.

2

What form of knowledge has practically become the rule in the human sciences? The first point is fairly obvious: the expert in the human sciences is a scientist, and science distinguishes itself and separates itself from nonscientific disciplines by its method. The expert is a man with a method; he is armed with a point of view (the point of view of science in general and of his science in particular) and with a set of tools (scientific techniques). The next question is more tricky: where does the scientific method, as applied to human things, begin and end? Here there are many difficulties and no agreement has been reached. But beyond these divergences and uncertainties—scientistic reason knows that it is the best, but it has some difficulty agreeing on just what it is—it is possible to make out the first commandments that, in a very general way, govern research taken to be "scientific," in other words, the fundamental rules of method. There are four such rules: exteriority, neutrality, technicity, and generality. In applying these rules, the scientist adopts a new way of looking at the world, a way that is foreign to the ordinary person as well as to the philosopher: the scientific viewpoint.

The first rule is that of *exteriority*. The expert situates himself out of bounds; he studies human affairs, but he is not involved—he keeps his distance. He separates himself from those he studies; he breaks with their way of thinking (common sense); he has no part either in their interests or their feelings; he adopts an exterior and superior point of view that does not implicate him as a person. He does not speak; science speaks through him. His point of view is impersonal; as a human being, he is not in question.

Plato and the Greeks after him understood thinking as a way of being. All authentic thought is a spiritual exercise, a quest in which the thinking subject is formed and transformed. There is no true knowledge except where man thinks with his whole being, where he commits himself fully. The expert shrugs his shoulders; he knows that science leaves him to himself, that he is expected only to lend, not to give himself. Holed up in his observatory, he is safe and warm, but his look is cold.

The human sciences are the study of human beings by human beings, but there is a distinction between them: on the one side is the ordinary person, a human being as human being; on the other is the scientist, someone who has renounced the natural form of human thinking and is thus not entirely human.

The second rule, that of *neutrality*, is in part a corollary of the first, and it tends in the same direction: it amputates thought. Neutrality forbids all judgment in the metaphysical, moral, and aesthetic domains. Questions of this order escape scientific reason and are relegated to outer darkness. As a result, the expert takes the world as given, he is surprised by nothing, he does not question existence, he renounces the search for meaning. His object is the laws by which human life functions, which he attempts to discern while abstaining from all "value judgments" on actions or works. Knowledge must remain "immaculate," to use Nietzsche's expression. This procedure breaks with the natural course of human reflection, that of the ordinary person as well as that of classical thought. When Aristotle observes and classifies political regimes, he has no other goal but to distinguish good and bad regimes. Otherwise, why and by virtue of what might one classify them? When Tocqueville analyzes "democratic" society, his concerns for freedom and for the quality of human life are constantly on his mind. If knowledge is indifferent to man's well-being, then why devote oneself to knowledge? "These questions are beside the point," answers the expert. "Method commands the suspension of reflection as soon as 'values' are in question. When the sociologist distinguishes types of families he has no business asking whether one type is better than another, and when he classifies works of art, he is not concerned with what art is. . . . Non possumus." This attitude, as Leo Strauss noted, would have seemed to the Greeks just as sensible as that of a shoemaker who refused to distinguish between good and bad shoes or of a doctor who refused to distinguish between health and sickness.

The third rule is that of *technicity*. Scientific knowledge must be authenticated by certain techniques that guarantee its validity, techniques of observation, inquiry, and verification that are held to be neutral and require only expertise. Techniques are the impersonal instruments of an impersonal knowledge. The production, verification, and transmission of knowledge are independent of the human qualities of the thinking subject; they call for no personal development. They require only the mastery of techniques, the mastery of the "problematic," and the cold attitude of the technician. The expert never goes anywhere without his toolbox. The more he uses expert methods, and the more he relies upon mathematics and computers, the more closely he approaches the "exact" sciences and gives scientific cachet to his work. The ideal would be to put the whole human experience in numbers and equations.[2]

Tocqueville respected this rule no more than the preceding ones. He did not make use of attitude scaling, public opinion surveys, or logarithmic tables; rather, he observed carefully, reflected a great deal, and spent some time every day with Pascal, Montesquieu, and Rousseau; he thought with his whole being and strove to understand from the inside. And he was much more intelligent than we are. ("What are you saying!" the expert interrupts, "Tocqueville was an amateur.")

Finally, the last rule: the human sciences aim at *generality*. Science by nature strives to reduce otherness to sameness, to eliminate particularities, to conquer diversity by establishing laws. But to eliminate uniqueness in the domain of the human sciences is not the same as to do it in the domain of the "exact" sciences. Is a man identical to another in the same way that a shellfish is identical to another shellfish? Is Caesar or Michelangelo reducible to any of his contemporaries in the same way that a given electron is reducible to any other electron? Culture brings to light the heterogeneity of the human world, but this heterogeneity is an obstacle to the rule of science: systems must be general in scope or they are no longer systems; laws must be generally applicable or they are no longer laws. The human sciences constitute a machine for producing abstract generalities in which the full breadth of humanity no longer has a place. "Vulgar people find no difference among men," Pascal wrote. Neither does science.

On the other hand, this suits the modern mind very well. Now knowledge has only to do with having; it is not a way of being. The expert does not stand out for his talents and intellectual virtues, but for the possession of a method, for a methodically impersonal way of thinking. "Write as if you were the first man," Rilke said; "Write as if you were not a man," says science. As a result, the richness of humanity, human experience, human qualities are without value for the understanding of man. The child psychologist has no children; no matter, he has method. The sociologist of love has never loved; no matter, he has method. The education specialist is emotionally disturbed; no matter, he has method. The economist is uncultivated; no problem, method will take care of everything. And yet "the world of scientific discovery is governed by an aristocracy of talent, not by a democracy of method."[3] If discoveries depended only upon method, "researchers" would never stop making discoveries. But the actual results are not so encouraging.

However this may be, method allows the expert to compartmentalize his existence: the categories in which he thinks are independent of those in which he lives. The expert is a modern man; he preserves his autonomy. He takes on no responsibilities, he simply exercises a function. In his domain, he is a technician of thought; otherwise, he enjoys the same indeterminate freedom as everyone else.

3

Knowledge is not within the province of being and it has nothing to say about being. Contemporary science, consistent with the duty of neutrality, has joined hands with equality by default in order to complete the great schism issuing from late modernity: the separation of knowledge and life. In every manual of the human sciences, or almost every one of them, one finds this golden rule: science never expresses any "value judgments." The world of "values" is foreign to logical or experimental reason—how is it possible to demonstrate, to verify, or to refute a moral imperative or an aesthetic judgment? Thus the human sciences do more than abdicate: they in fact teach the arbitrariness of "values," they promote relativism. Every "preference," be it perverse or mad, must be considered as just as legitimate as any other before the bar of reason. Selection among "values" is a matter of pure subjectivity: *de gustibus non est disputandum*. In other words, the science of scientists lends its full legitimacy to the fundamental doctrine of equality by default: there is no hierarchy in the domain of being. Modern thought, through the voice of scientific reason, abandons vital questions to opinion; it renounces meaning and says that all meaning is arbitrary.

In this way method filters one's view of the world; it crushes vital differences and prevents the telling of how things are, of calling things by their names. Here, for example, is what Beaumarchais' Figaro (in *The Marriage of Figaro*) might say concerning the censorship imposed by the rule of scientific neutrality:

> If, as a jurist, I do not distinguish between a true and a false constitution, between the penal code of a tyrant and that of a liberal, between racial laws and others; if, as a political scientist, I see no difference between force and violence, skill and cunning, the statesman and the demagogue, a healthy and a corrupt people; if, as a linguist, I refuse to rank the language of Racine and the gibberish of the expert; if, as a sociologist of art, I consider a casual painter to be equivalent to Leonardo de Vinci, the Parthenon to a Nambikwara or Bororo hut, Mozart's music to Michael Jackson's; if, as an educationist, I close my eyes to intelligence and stupidity, effort and laziness, politeness and rudeness; if, as a sociologist of "sexual relations," I do not allow myself to distinguish between relations that unite (or disunite) Abraham and Sarah, the harlot and her client, Tristan and Isolde, or the Marquis de Sade and his victims; if, as a family expert, I say nothing of tenderness, of jeal-

ousy, of devotion, of egoism, of purity, of conceit, of
trust, of perversion, of faithfulness, of vanity, of gen-
erosity, of guilt, of forgiveness; if, as a religious studies
scientist, I do not raise the question of the existence of
God (hardly an appropriate question); if, as a thinking
man, I condemn myself to ignorance concerning what
matters and what matters little (by what standard could
I tell?); if, as a man of science, I renounce any thought
of justifying science; if, as one committed to the science
of man, I renounce all consideration of the greatness
and the misery of man; then I can write freely and
learnedly, subject to the supervision of my colleagues.

4

Science therefore knows only ordinary men and men deprived of
any natural purposes. But it must go further. Even such an ampu-
tated human being still remains a troublemaker recalcitrant to the
rules of method. The main problem has to do with this commonplace reflection: the human being is opaque. The reasons behind
human action are invisible, as are all the ways in which a human
being is more than his actions. The hidden side of man, his internal
life, is what literature unveils. But for science this internal life is an
obstacle. How can an external, impersonal point of view grasp the
inner life? How is it possible to demonstrate, validate, even quantify
what takes place in the human heart? And how can this be subjected
to scientific order, to those laws which are the objective of science?

What is to be done? The only solution is to eliminate human
consciousness or reduce it to some elementary data. In the first case,
man is seen as the product of external determinations, the uncon-
scious agent of forces that surpass him; in the second, he becomes a
being whose desires are driven by some elementary psychological
force (sexual desire, utilitarian rationality). One or the other of these
two kinds of interpretations underlies sociologism, economism,
behaviorism, Freudianism, structuralism, and culturalism—a kalei-

doscope of interpretations of man, the common theme of which does him little honor. Method tends to have an abasing effect: All human beings are equally empty, or almost. All individuals are alike in their absence of being.

Experts thus work, whether they realize it or not, for equality by default. They do not explore what is real, but substitute for the real world inhabited by beings of flesh and blood an artificial world, laden with abstractions and devoid of substance, a flattened world, a homogeneous world. This vision is false, but the more it is taken for true, the more it becomes true. To the extent that this substitute world holds sway over human consciousness, the substitution becomes part of reality. The dominant human sciences misunderstand the human world, and they tend to transform this world according to their misunderstanding.

CHAPTER 6
PÉGUY AND THE ECONOMIST

1

Consider the case of a contemporary economist, a cutting-edge economist—a person highly qualified in his specialty (say, a certain very specific aspect of market theory), recognized by his peers, esteemed for his work. Every day, at his office or in his classes, he puts on the eyeglasses of economic science and dons the apparel of the economist. In so doing, he transforms his identity: he is no longer the being of flesh and blood known to his family and friends, the person who maintains vital relations with other beings of flesh and blood; he is metamorphosed into this separate being known as the pure specialist, the expert with the cold look, armed with the scientific method, who now sees the world only through the filter of his specialty. At work he is an economist and only an economist; he withdraws and isolates himself. On the one hand, he strips himself of all he knows as a human being and separates himself from ordinary people and from the ordinary person he otherwise is. On the other, he breaks with culture and accords no interest to the other human sciences. The economic point of view suffices unto itself.

As an economist, our hero thus has need of no one other than his colleagues in economics who generally share the same viewpoint. Among economists, this much is clear: the science of economics (which has taken the place of the old political economy) is a modern, "scientific" discipline, free of all encumbrances; it must have complete independence. How can one take seriously the tradition inherited from Aristotle according to which economics is by nature subordinate, that it has no other purpose than the *good life* of human beings, and that consequently the science of economics is a moral and political science? What a confusion of genres! What business here has a concept like "the good life," which has nothing to do with economics? Economics is the mistress of its own realm; it constructs by abstraction its own proper domain and defines its own end: the optimal usage of scarce productive resources. In other words, the economy is a technical tool in the service of economic efficiency, measured appropriately, that is to say in quantities, quantities of consumption (and combined as needed with certain rules of equity).[1] This technique is very sophisticated indeed, thanks in particular to the use of mathematics and computers, which makes it possible to multiply models and to endlessly refine theories.

Our man is thus a pure economist and as such a pure scientist, clothed in immaculate white. He adopts the neutral and impersonal attitude required by the method, dutifully ignoring vital questions and replacing traditional distinctions with distinctions corresponding to his point of view, economic distinctions. On the one hand, he isolates his subject matter from all other human activities and no longer sees human beings except as economic agents; true to his obligations as a specialist, his objects of study are not humans but fractions of humans. On the other hand, he limits his purview to what the rules of the method allow him to see, thus mutilating himself in the service of science, thinking with only a part of himself. He is a fraction of a man who occupies himself with fractions of other men.

Now consider Charles Péguy, the very opposite of an expert, a man committed wholly to what he is doing and who does not put the slightest distance between his thought and his life, a man who takes every risk and never gives up—a poet and a philosopher, armed not with an impersonal method but with the spirit of simplicity, of wonder, of a childlike spirit about which he has written such beautiful pages and which is the soul of his poetry. For him, the essential has nothing to do with techniques. It consists in looking at the world in the right way, in submitting oneself to what is real, in not showing off, in being prepared to be surprised and to admire, in not being systematic, in saying what one sees. Péguy does not equip himself with an a priori viewpoint; he positions himself to listen faithfully, piously to reality, and he puts his whole heart into giving voice to its richness, its breadth. Under his pen, vital distinctions come to life; he is constantly distinguishing what matters from what does not, what is worthy from what is not, what gives life and what desiccates it. With what eloquence, with what insistence he explores profound joys, intense moments, authentic conduct, in order to make great works sing, to oppose true geniuses to petty authorities, living knowledge to dead . . .

"Living knowledge" for Péguy consists of culture and memory, the treasure of great works and the ever-present past; "dead knowledge" means the new human sciences that had conquered the Sorbonne. Between these two forms of knowledge war had been declared. I refer to the famous quarrel of the "new Sorbonne" in which Péguy engaged himself with ardor and vehemence, sparing no pains in taking up the defense of the humanities and denouncing the new masters—sociologists, historians, critics—who petrified reality and abased men in the name of science and method. Those professors who do not feel the intensity of history, art, and life, who have no access to what shimmers in the event, the act, or the work, are like the blind leading the blind, he wrote. But Péguy's blows did not shake the walls of the "new Sorbonne," and its masters have produced many offspring. Our economist may be said to be one of them.

The world that Péguy brings to light is poles apart from that of our economist. Péguy submits himself to the way things are and points up vital differences; the economist submits things to a point of view that effaces and crushes vital differences. Péguy is the adversary par excellence of equality by default; the economist, consciously or not, belongs to the other camp.

2

"In my time," Péguy writes,

> everyone sang (except for me, but I was already
> unworthy of being part of that era). In most kinds of
> work people sang. Today we grumble. . . . Can you
> believe. . . that we knew workers who in the morning
> thought only of working? They got up in the
> morning—and how early they got up!—and they sang
> to think that they were going to work. At eleven
> o'clock, they sang as they went for their soup. In sum,
> it's always as in Hugo; we must always go back to Hugo:
> *ils allaient, ils chantaient* (they went off singing). To
> work was their greatest joy, the taproot of their being.
> And the reason of their being. There was an unbeliev-
> able honor accorded work, the most beautiful of all
> honors, the most Christian, the only one perhaps that
> holds up. This is why, for example, I say that a free-
> thinker of that time was more Christian than a devout
> person of our day—because a devout person of our day
> is necessarily a bourgeois. And now everyone is bour-
> geois.
>
> We had a sense of the honor of work exactly like that
> which governed the hand and the heart in the Middle
> Ages; it was the same meaning preserved intact under-
> neath. We understood this care pushed to perfection,
> from the smallest detail to the whole. We understood
> this piety of *work well done* pushed and sustained up to
> its most extreme requirements. Throughout all my
> childhood I saw chairs reseated with straw in exactly the
> same spirit and with the same heart that these same
> people had hewn their cathedrals.[2]

The economist remains cold as ice: "All that is nothing but literature. Whether people sing or not has no economic significance. Whatever Péguy may say, work is a factor of production, which is a matter of economic rationality just as capital is: its characteristics are a price, a level of productivity, an opportunity cost. . . . Scientific calculations, not fine sentiments, determine the optimal combination of factors. What was the value added at the time celebrated by this text? Would you want to go back to the age of cathedrals? Neither nostalgia nor moralism ever put food on the table."

From a strictly economic point of view, the economist is right. He is also right to criticize a moralism in which the display of elevated sentiments goes along with indifference to concrete situations. But Péguy is in no way subject to this critique. Son of the people (*le peuple*) and proud of it, his feet are always solidly on the ground, and while at the helm of the journal *Cahiers de la Quinzaine* he devoted years of long days to the labor of publishing. He knew the meaning of a shortfall in accounts, of difficult ends of the month, of the uncertainty of tomorrow; he experienced in his flesh "that economic life is the indispensable support of mental life."[3] Disdain for material questions was altogether foreign to Péguy.

Where then is the stumbling block? Unlike the economist in his office (rather, in front of his computer), Péguy does not reduce the man at work to the status of an economic agent; he focuses on real people, on the way they live and what they do. The economic point of view severs work from its subjective dimension; it subordinates it to the merely economic ends of the economy. Instrumentalized, work has no value other than its contribution to created wealth; it is a homogeneous and quantifiable activity (a matter of differences of degree and not of nature) by which man produces goods and services. That man might himself be implicated in his work, that he might flourish or degrade himself in it, is beside the point. No matter the honor of work of which Péguy speaks, no matter that a given activity be worthy or unworthy, that it elevate or alienate— such considerations mean nothing to economic calculation. Vital distinctions are effaced.

To give an extreme example, there is the distinction between free labor and that of slaves. The difference is only one of degree: forced labor is not very productive. From the point of view of economic rationality, free cooperation is better than the enslavement of human beings, since it is more profitable or, if you like, since it increases the productivity of human capital. A case study consisting of an economic analysis of Buchenwald or Dachau would confirm this empirically.

Also effaced is the distinction between honorable and dishonorable work: there is no difference between an honest man and a charlatan, between legitimate interest and greed. The manufacturing of medicines is on a par with the production of illegal drugs (when account is taken of the fact that the latter belongs to the informal economy); both the doctor and the drug dealer belong to the service economy, just as do the fortune-teller and the economics professor. Cheating enters into the equation only to the extent that it carries an economic cost; the rest doesn't count. And yet the moral meaning of actions weighs on the feelings of the actors. It is not a matter of indifference to the economist whether he gains in prestige by sound research or by forgery. Would he not be outraged if he were suspected of rigging his statistics? Does it not matter then to others whether a livelihood is earned by cheating or honestly? Or must we consider the economist as a special case, the only person with a moral conscience?

Finally, what disappears is the distinction between a craft or trade and a mere job [between *le métier* and *la function*], between work that has a creative aspect and fragmented drudge work. For work to have its true meaning, it is essential to maintain an equilibrium between the creative and the merely laborious elements. But the economist pays no attention to this: to him it matters little that crafts disappear, that work is broken up into a myriad of micro-functions that are nothing but drudgery, as long as the efficiency of labor is thereby enhanced. Consumers benefit; producers will have to make do. But does this trade-off always make sense? According to Péguy, workers once

knew that in every life which would be by definition a
life of work, the taste and appetite for work are like the
taste for bread in the economy of the meal. When the
taste for bread is gone, no drug can do anything to
make up for it. When the taste and appetite for work
are gone, no demagogic drug has ever been able to make
up for it.[4]

3

"The greatest work of genius," Péguy writes, "is passed on to our
feeble hands."

In our hands, in our care, by our hands alone, it receives
an ever incomplete fulfillment. One reading of ours
completes or corrupts this *Antigone*; one reading of ours
crowns or uncrowns this achievement of Homer, this
Iliad and this *Odyssey*. . . . It is frightening, my friend,
to think that we have every license, that we have the
exorbitant right to give a bad reading of Homer, to
uncrown a work of genius, that the greatest work of the
greatest genius is delivered into our hands, not inert but
living like a little wild rabbit. And especially that by let-
ting it fall from our hands, we can by forgetfulness put
it to death. What an appalling risk, my friend, what an
appalling adventure; and especially, what a frightening
responsibility.[5]

The economist shrugs: "These observations, like the preceding
ones, have no meaning from an economic point of view, or more
generally from a scientific viewpoint. Péguy distinguishes and celebrates those works that he qualifies as works of genius, as he is free
to do. But in the name of what does he proclaim a general responsibility? Why would his judgment or that of past ages be valid for
someone else? Scientific reason is neutral; it takes individual preferences as it finds them. The death of Homer would mean that indi-

viduals have found more satisfactions elsewhere. Who can complain? Whoever questions the judgment of the market questions the judgment of the public. The same rule—the law of supply and demand—applies to all private goods, so why should literature deserve special treatment?"

From the economic point of view, goods are homogeneous; there is no difference in nature between the market for books and the market for cat food or weapons, no difference between the markets that deal in art, sports, or organs of the human body. The individual consumer is king—by what right may his choices be limited? The logic of economic calculation leads to what Péguy called a world "universally prostituted because universally interchangeable."[6] Money becomes the universal standard; all is measurable, interchangeable, substitutable—all is homogeneous.

Goods are homogeneous because preferences are homogeneous. The economist serves the utility (or the satisfaction derived from consumption) of economic agents, and utility rises with the quantity of consumption (to the point of satiety). What is consumed can only be distinguished in terms of more or less; it is universally subject to the same quantitative rules: more is better, the quantity of better declines with the quantity of more. The a prioris of method prohibit the slightest criterion of quality; the economist limits himself to registering the arbitrary diversity of tastes. In other words, he consecrates the rule of individual subjectivity while reducing human subjectivity to a rudimentary rational mechanics accounted for in numbers and curves. One result, for example, is the following: take a young man who hesitates between *The Odyssey* and a pornographic video—what is the best choice? There can be no doubt as to the response: the rational choice, the one that allows the maximization of utility, is determined by the law of equalizing marginal utilities adjusted for price.[7] Or take a drunk who is trying to sober up: he is tempted, he hesitates, the economist comes to his aid and explains to him the law of declining marginal utility (the utility of an additional unit of a product declines along with the quantity consumed)—maybe it is the effect of the drink, but the alcoholic has difficulty following. Or take a kid who puts all his pocket money into the electronic games he avidly plays to the point of deadening his mind—the choice is economically rational. Or take a man who is offered a mess of pottage in exchange for his freedom—the choice again is a matter of calculation.

The economist takes no account of the nature of economic goods, any more than of free goods. Wealth and poverty, the optimum and the rational, growth and national product, standard of living and utility have nothing to do with what is beyond the world of the market. But the GNP cannot account for services furnished by mothers to their families—"your remark is beside the point, since these are nonmarket services." Consider another example: what if ugliness and boredom increase with productivity—"I do not deal with such matters." Or what if too much economic rationality undoes social bonds and isolates human beings—"Why do you persist? I tell you that this is none of my affair." But what if the gap widens between what is good economically and what is good for humans as humans—"I choose not to answer you."

Thus, except in the extreme case of poverty, in which the economic factor is paramount, the economist amputates the real life of human beings, in particular what Burke called the "unbought grace of life," of which Péguy spoke so eloquently:

> The contentment, the simple contentment of the heart
> and of the arms, the contentment and enjoyment of the
> hands, all happiness, all that makes up the happiness
> and the joy of the good worker, of simple workers: to eat
> a good steaming soup under the web-like illumination
> of the familial lamp, seated at the common round table,
> slightly oval, before his simple human wife, among
> magnificent jostling children.[8]

4

Such examples could be multiplied. The powerful machinery of the science of economics ceaselessly crushes differences that matter, including the differences among social bonds. What is a society as seen through the prism of economics today? A collection of economic agents, an aggregate of producers and consumers, a web of human relations reduced to utilitarian and impersonal relations, leaving only the weakest bonds among human beings. Who would risk his life to defend the market? Economic analysis "desocializes" men; it misunderstands what true social bonds are, the bonds that engage the heart and cement families, institutions, nations.

Also effaced are all vital distinctions relative to time: the time of the economist, like everything else, is homogeneous; it forms a uniformly divisible continuum. But in a full and whole life, things happen quite differently: individual existence gives rise to alternations between times of intensity and times of flatness, as in history there are "epochs" and "periods" (Péguy). There is a time for every thing, good and bad times, rhythms that must be respected in ordering one's life and giving honor where it is due. That's beside the point, the economist interrupts: let us speak instead of the irrational rule that breaks the uniformity of economic time and prohibits work on Sunday.

Finally, vital differences among individuals are effaced. For the economist, all human beings are alike, not of course because they have some higher calling in common but because they all rationally pursue objectives that are equally irrational. *Homo economicus* is cold, rational, and utilitarian; he is gifted in calculating but empty of substance. Human beings are indistinguishable in their way of being; they can only be distinguished by their incomes, their levels of consumption or productivity. Here, everything that Péguy loves, all that he celebrates—good manners and morals, fine workmanship, beautiful language, simple joys, bonds of the flesh, the honor of the poor, the genius of Homer—none of this has any meaning. We are indeed in the world of equality by default.

5

Our economist has shown great patience. Now, suddenly, he speaks out: "You're not giving me a fair hearing. Your whole argument rests on a basic mistake: you blame me in effect for not dealing with what interests you. Have you never heard of scientific specialization and of the rules of scientific method? It has never been my ambition to clarify what you call 'real life'; I claim only to analyze a specific object, constructed and isolated by abstraction, and to analyze it scientifically without prejudice and without any kind of judgment having to do with values. Must I remind you that scientific reason is neutral, for the very good reason that it is impossible scientifically to demonstrate a value judgment? So there, that is my position; I am a scientist, a specialist, and my point of view is that of a specialist. Why do you insist that I get involved with questions that you call vital and concerning which any scientist worthy of the name must declare himself incompetent? Read Péguy if that does something for you—I'm not concerned with your tastes—but let me work in peace. And let me add finally that as an economist what your poet has to say, in prose or in verse, is the least of my concerns. Is that clear enough?"

Indeed. Like every specialist isolated in his specialty, the economist plays the role of Pontius Pilate. But he does more than this; he locks himself inside certain dilemmas and fails to account for his own practice:

1. The science of economics is no more neutral than any other human activity. Why devote oneself to the scientific analysis of the economy? The economist is bound to silence, since as a scientist he refuses to engage in "value judgments." And what justifies this prohibition against "value judgments"? The economist cannot respond to this either, since the answer is inadmissible: the value of scientific knowledge, that is, a "value judgment." The economist implicitly takes the science of economics to be good, but he cannot account for what he does. To be consistent, he should, for example, speak to his students as follows: "I am going to teach you economics. But if

you ask me if this science is to be preferred to ignorance, or an efficient economy to banditry on a grand scale, this is beyond my competence. Don't ask me further to justify my work as a professor or the values on which the university rests; such questions are beyond our subject matter."

2. As a specialist, the economist can say what is important from his point of view, but not whether his point of view is important. He devotes his professional life to an intellectual activity defined by a subject matter the importance of which is a question he cannot even address. He must have some notion in the back of his head—what treatise of economics begins with these words: "Here are a thousand pages of science applied to economics. Whether this has any importance or significance, who can say? Ask someone else"?

3. Economic science aims at efficiency in the service of individual preferences. This choice is in no way "scientific." If it introduces a criterion of justice, again this has no scientific basis. The economist is once again in the grip of unavowed internal contradictions.

4. The science of economics imposes a filter on reality. It equips itself with a particular viewpoint, severs its object, and creates a vacuum around it. "It is my right as a scientist," says the economist. But why does he not add, "This highly scientific point of view has the effect of substituting a world constructed according to the needs of science for the real world; this new world is artificial and is populated by men who are artificial and artificially cut off from everything else. I know nothing of religion, I ignore politics, I set aside customs, I erase membership groups, I suppress feelings, I deny morality—on this scorched earth science flourishes. But quite clearly one must not ask it to give an account of real economic life, not to mention real life simply." But to say this is obviously to raise a commonsensical question: why then should one study economics in this way? Is there not a constitutional defect in the official viewpoint of economic science in that, instead of submitting to the structures inherent in reality, it attempts to impose an artificial framework on it? The wisdom of the good cook of whom Plato

speaks consisted in knowing that one must cut up a fowl not by arming oneself with an a priori method but by following the contours of the fowl. Maybe the science of economics is designed only for the satisfaction of economists. (In terms of general economic analysis, such a choice would be rational.)

In practice, the contemporary economist who accepts the rules of the game engages in economism just as Mr. Jourdain, in Molière's *Le Bougeois Gentilhomme*, made prose: naturally, spontaneously, he sets up the economic point of view as the privileged way of looking at the world. Economics sees itself as "the queen of the social sciences"; it considers itself the most scientific (long live mathematics!); it is the most decorated (the only one to be honored by a Nobel Prize), the most recognized, also the most victorious. No doubt within economics there are various contradictory tendencies and heretical views. But taken as a whole economics presents itself as a powerful machine in the service of economism—and equality by default. Under the mantel of science, it assumes and in a way consecrates a world in which human beings are equal in their lack of being, and within this framework it does its best to make men adapt to economism, rather than make the economy adapt to men. It tends to transform the world according to its narrow vision.

6

Let there be no mistake: our economist is no firebrand. In fact he stands out as a moderate in that he confines himself to properly economic questions. But the army of economists includes more advanced battalions: these are the adepts of a generalized economics who, armed with economic concepts, set out to conquer social life as a whole.[9] *Homo economicus*, rationality, and utility take on a universal significance, and economic analysis is applied everywhere and always, as long as scarcity exists. What then becomes of politics? It is nothing more than a market where collective services or promises of collective services are exchanged against ballots, a commerce analogous to what happens in the mercantile sphere. What becomes of marriage? A rational matter determined by calculations of costs and benefits adjusted for probabilities, which reminds one of what Engels wrote on "marriages of convenience": the wife is distinct from the courtesan only by the fact that she sells herself only once. What becomes of procreation, crime, suicide? Nothing but rational and utilitarian acts to be accounted for by economic calculations supported by massive numbers of curves and equations. Some such studies have pushed analytical finesse to the point of defining an "optimal level of criminality" (measured by equalizing the marginal social costs of crime and the marginal social costs of its prevention), or demonstrating the rationality of commerce in newborns or an abortion market.

Thus humanity becomes a homogeneous whole. People are all the same in all situations, that is, always and everywhere rational and utilitarian, that is, rational and egoistic.[10] Here one attains the extreme form of the effacement of vital differences, *the extreme form of the homogenization of the world*. The voter is the same as the consumer (although, if he were rational, would he bother to vote when his vote would in no way affect the final result?), the statesman is the same as the speculator (although, if this were the case, no unpopular measure would ever be taken, nor any long-term measure), the soldier as the gangster (except that he calculates badly), the economist as the pimp (but does he calculate as well?). There is no difference in kind between buying apples and having a child, betting on races or committing suicide, organizing pedophile orgies or preparing a colloquium on economics. The same interpretation holds for the construction of cathedrals and for that of gas ovens, for those who saved Jews during the last world war and for those who turned them in, for torturers and for their victims. The sacrifice of Péguy, killed by a bullet in the forehead, means the same as an act of desertion; Joan of Arc is made of the same stuff as Stalin—is it necessary to extend the list any further? As Orwell noted, some opinions are so stupid that only intellectuals can believe them.

If these imperialists of economics, intoxicated by their learned constructions, were right, Péguy would have understood nothing concerning what is a human being. Nor would Dante, nor Shakespeare, nor Racine, nor the other great writers who were weak enough to believe that man is a complicated and divided being who cannot be reduced to egoistic calculations. It would be necessary to rewrite all the great works—for example *Polyeucte,* in which Pauline, finally illuminated by the grace of the science of economics, might speak as follows (Corneille, forgive us):

> I see, I know, I believe, I am disabused.
> Calculation rules all, to the point of satiety.
> If Polyeucte loved me, it was out of self-interest,
> If he gives me up for God, it is for the sake of utility.[11]

Finally, if these economists were right, their own analyses would have to be explained not by a concern for truth but by their personal interests as professional economists. We will not insult them by taking them at their word. But we wish for them the earliest departure from that "kingdom of disgrace" of which Péguy speaks, that in which one does not even know whereof one speaks.

CHAPTER 7
THE WORLD AT OUR DISPOSAL

The scientism dominant in the human sciences has the perverse power of transforming the best fellow in the world into an icy, impersonal, irresponsible person. At the other extreme, it gives arms to the will to power at the same time it covers it with the veil of neutrality. To be sure, all technicians of knowledge are not cut from the same cloth; still, they form a powerful army that marches, in dispersed ranks, under the brilliant banner of science. In the first ranks, so to speak, one finds the certified "scientific researchers" who hold influential positions in universities and research institutes and who have never been so numerous. Whoever visits a large university library in Europe or the United States with fresh eyes (eyes not blinded by familiarity or method) cannot help but be taken aback. What a flood of technoscientistic books and journals devoted to human affairs, compared with the little space taken up by humanistic learning! Computers sate you with "scientific" references— enough easily to write up impressive bibliographies—and you face shelves lined with battalions of "scientific" journals. If it is true that this intellectual activity is misguided, then what a waste of effort! Still worse, what effort spent to cover the world with darkness!

The growing hold of modern knowledge not only concerns intellectual life *stricto sensu*; it concerns everyone's way of seeing and acting. More or less consciously, scientistic science tends to change radically the way people look at the world. The experts in human sciences, in particular, "deconstruct" the world of real life, the world deepened and broadened by culture, and they construct another world filtered through method. They create an artificial world and tend to impose it as the true world. This work is far advanced, and it is revealed in our language. The human sciences have created a new language that may be spoken in French as well as in English or German—an artificial language for an artificial world.

1

Andromache appears. Pyrrhus, who had replied haughtily to the entreaties of Orestes' mission, suddenly changes tone: "Were you looking for me, madame? Might I allow myself such a charming hope?"[1] The answer that Andromache then gives marvelously illustrates, by its sober intensity and layers of meaning, the perfection of Racine's language:

> Je passais jusqu'au lieu où l'on garde mon fils,
> Puisque une fois le jour vous souffrez que je voie
> Le seul bien qui me reste et d'Hector et de Troie
> Je ne l'ai point encore embrassé aujourd'hui.

But if Andromache spoke in today's scientific fashion her reply would take quite a different form. For example: "The situation of objective incarceration of which you are the organizing agent authorizes, apropos of the management of my schedule, only one daily contact with the remainder of my familial environment and of my sociocultural milieu. My motivation, in effectuating this relational process, was to express with him my unfortunate experience."

It is not only that such language might well make us wince, whereas Racine's sings to our ears; the modern vocabulary also mutilates meaning. Racine's great style gives texture to things; it bespeaks the intensity of the event, the power of feelings; it lets us hear the beating of the heart. The heavy and cold style of the language contaminated by the human sciences, on the contrary, flattens reality; it tends inherently to smother life. The words of Racine are simple and concrete. They have an evocative power fully exploited in the admirable art of composition possessed by the author of *Andromache*. On the other hand, the new vocabulary is complicated and abstract; it comes from somewhere outside, somewhere foreign to human experience, and is thus unsuited to giving voice to living reality.

What then is the message of this language? It reorders the world and replaces vital distinctions with new categories that run roughshod over actual ways of being. Let us consider the main categories of the new language, which can be grouped under four rubrics: the language of the indeterminate self that comes from psychology; the language of undifferentiated social life that comes from sociology; the language of man as a function that comes from economics; and finally the language of history as impersonal mechanics that comes from the social sciences as a whole.

1. *The language of the indeterminate self.* Allan Bloom tells the story of a taxi driver in Atlanta who, a few years ago, explained to him all the benefits he had derived from the psychotherapy he had received while imprisoned for dealing drugs: he had found his identity and learned to love himself, he said.[2] Modern psychology is devoted to "self-expression"; it is perfectly attuned to modern equality, and its vocabulary has largely moved into common speech: *motivation, identity, creativity, fantasy, values,* as well as all the compound words that use the prefix "self": *self-expression, self-esteem, self-acceptance, self-confidence,* and so on. On all the talk shows that plague American television screens the new magical formulas resonate: "Express yourself," "I have increased my self-esteem," "Be who you are." In France, analogous expressions have also become very popular: "I embrace myself just as I am"; "I live my fantasies," and so forth. Everywhere advertisers nudge consumers in the same direction. The area where our way of talking has changed most rad-

ically is doubtless that of physical love. Henceforth, the proper tone and words are those of the expert: one speaks, coldly, of "sexual relations" between "partners," of "sexual orientation," of "sexual minorities"; one hardly speaks of love, and one ignores all rules of conduct with the exception that when medicine gives orders, it's serious business—for that is a matter of technical expertise.

This is the vocabulary of indeterminate freedom, of the Self without substance. "I actualize myself," says modern man, "in the name of my own values." But is it a matter of indifference whether one "actualizes oneself" after the fashion of Diafoirus (the ignorant and pedantic doctor of Molière's *Malade imaginaire*) or Tartuffe (the consummate hypocrite whom Molière portrays unforgettably in the play by the same name), or, alternatively, according to the example of Rodrigue (the young hero of Corneille's *Le Cid*) or Esther (the biblical heroine who inspired Racine)? Must we believe that the cannibal, the necrophiliac, the drug addict are only following "their own values"? All these empty categories, having no specific content, serve only to give an appearance of justification to "all is permitted," or "I do as I like." The ideas of responsibility, moral failing, transgression, and all the distinctions borne by the language of sentiments elaborated and refined over centuries—distinctions between pleasure and joy, for example, or between desire and will, conceit and pride, audacity and courage, envy and jealousy, humility and modesty, pharisaism and tartuffery—tend to be obliterated.

2. *The language of undifferentiated social life.* Like those just discussed, categories inherited from sociology introduce distinctions without really distinguishing things. This is the procedure: the new categories carve up real heterogeneous wholes and lump together what classical learning distinguished. *Culture, ideology, organization, communication, mobilization, resources, message, sacred, deviance*—so many words which, in the hands of sociologists, show the same tendency: these are "catch-all" words. Culture as understood traditionally distinguishes great works; in the vocabulary forged by experts and popularized by subexperts, it generally refers to a vast jumble

THE WORLD AT OUR DISPOSAL

wherein all cultural productions or cultural practices are thrown together—Racine side by side with rock singers and Tocqueville with the tabloid press. Similarly, the word *organization* lumps together the family and the prison, the learned association and the insane asylum. The word *communication* tends to assimilate the sales pitch with philosophical midwifery, propaganda with education. The term *deviance* operates analogously: Christians in Nero's empire were deviants, just as were criminals (which is doubtless why the Christians were treated as such), and dissidents in the Soviet Union were deviants just as were the insane (which is doubtless why the dissidents were confined in asylums). And so on with the other terms.[3]

Today sociological vocabulary informs public discourse. It impresses and seduces those who want to impress. With such a vocabulary, Tocqueville would never have been able to deepen the analysis of modern society.

3. *The language of man as a function,* that is, the language of the science of economics, has also become commonplace among politicians, journalists, and administrators. As we have seen, economics has declared its autonomy and in so doing has made its categories autonomous. This particular and fragmentary point of view has claimed a self-sufficiency. The more this autonomous and exclusionary economic vocabulary spreads, the more the economic vision of the world prevails.[4]

4. *The language of history as an impersonal mechanism* has also become an integral part of the "official" language of modern societies. *Process, dynamic, development, structures, systems, fields, mutation, social agents, social conditions*—all these are terms that may have (partial) validity, but whose unopposed usage suggests that the way the world works is purely anonymous and mechanical. "Social dynamics" has its laws such as the market, where man is the agent of social processes or economic mechanisms in whose meaning he does not knowingly participate; he may even be unaware of the very reasons behind his actions. This whole vocabulary tends in one

direction: history escapes human will; it develops according to its own laws. The failure of Marxism did not bring about that of historicism understood more broadly, because historicism is consubstantial with the social sciences insofar as they consider themselves scientific, and also because the spirit of equality finds it congenial (in that it puts all people at the same level, where no one plays a privileged role). From this perspective, politics fades away, and with it the vocabulary of statesmanship. There are good reasons for this: politics is the domain in which the few command the many with consequences for the destiny of all, a domain in which people have a greater or lesser importance according to whether they are leaders or led, the domain par excellence of human action in history.

It would clearly be absurd to deny that part of history escapes human intentions—especially since the analysis of emergent effects, positive or negative, is one of the rare incontestable contributions of contemporary social science.[5] But it would be just as absurd to reduce history to impersonal mechanics when the events of the twentieth century provide spectacular evidence to the contrary. Method must have a strangely blinding power in order for so many specialists to have managed to ignore the autonomy of politics and the role of human will in history in the century of Lenin, Mao, and Hitler (or, on the other hand, of Churchill, Franklin Roosevelt, de Gaulle, Ben-Gurion, or Jean Monnet). By presenting an impersonal vision of history, the social sciences denature reality, but they also influence it. They invite human beings to behave as if history were what they say it is. Their influence tends to vindicate their theories.

All these categories are the fruit of method or of makeshift theorizing inspired by method. They do not account for real experience but increasingly insinuate themselves between human beings and their experience. The human sciences erect a wall of general ideas that masks the living flesh of reality. Words are not neutral, even those which attempt to be. What is being inscribed in our language is a filter imposed on the world.

2

The new categories tend to replace distinctions inherited from Western civilization, and as such they bring a completely different world into view: a homogeneous and thus disordered world, a world abandoned to human irresponsibility.

Western civilization, as fashioned by Christianity and Greek philosophy, ordered the world and subordinated man to an order. Christianity replaced the Greek order of the Cosmos with the order of Creation; thus it confirmed the existence of a natural order consistent with the nature of man. Civilization fixed norms and set limits; it framed human activity, distinguishing between what is to be praised and blamed, what is decent and indecent, what is sacred and sacrilegious. It thus set limits on human action.

Equality by default radically subverts this order or, rather, these orders. Modern man, as we have seen, is sovereign and indeterminate. The sovereignty of man precludes a superhuman order, and his indeterminacy precludes a specifically human order. Human beings and their actions, experiences, and works are all put on the same level; the world is homogeneous, devoid of any vital order.

And what is the response of our scientists' science? They make the same case. The expert categories give order to the world only in appearance; they are in fact instruments of the homogenization of the world: the expressions of the Self do not admit of hierarchy; the forms of "culture," of "communication," of "organization" are all of the same nature, economic activities are only distinguished by differences of degree, and so on. The order of science gives no guidance to human action; it is not a human order because it is foreign to man's humanity. It offers only a false appearance of order to a world without order.

More than this, scientistic science puts itself at the service of modern freedom insofar as this freedom is a freedom without responsibility. The paradox is apparent: the pure, hard human sciences and the modern version of freedom no doubt have a common enemy—the being of man, or his substance—but how can the former serve the latter, since it tends to reduce or negate human freedom? This, it appears, can be articulated as follows: impersonal history says, "I work by rules that you do not control." Modern man deduces, "Very well, history goes on without me, I have no responsibility, I do as I like." Or, rather, "Very well, the process of history needs no justification, and my work is on the right side, so why question me as to some special responsibility?" The science of various determinisms extended to include individual acts says, "Man is what one makes of him." Modern man replies: "Very well, society is responsible, it doesn't concern me, all the more reason for me to do as I like."[6] The social sciences hardly trouble our individual awareness of freedom—to paraphrase Pascal, our awareness of individual freedom is invincible to all forms of determinism—but the social sciences work to emancipate this freedom from all responsibility; they contribute to the blind sovereignty of man over the world.

If everything is on the same level, if man has no particular responsibility, then the limits of human action disappear. *The homogeneous world is a world at our disposal.* If everything is homogeneous, everything is doable, everything is malleable, everything is fungible, everything is fit for public display. Nothing is given except the radical autonomy of the individual. The world is reduced to a field of maneuver or to a spectacle; it is delivered over to the irresponsible action of human beings. More precisely, it is delivered over to a practical reason the power of which is multiplied by technique, but which is purely instrumental and procedural. The outcome of this logic is that modern reason is a blindly advancing colossus.

PART TWO

THE IRRATIONAL
RATIONALIZATION
OF THE WORLD

CHAPTER 8
REASON, MCDONALD'S, AND BEING

1

Throughout the history of modern reason its status has undergone important changes. Once it was master, now it is only the servant or the master-servant. At its birth modern reason trumpeted the empire of reason, the reign of "Enlightenment," while discrediting its opponent by presenting it as the camp of prejudice, convention, and the principle of authority. If these formulations were polemical and overstated, they nevertheless expressed a real break. Of course modern thought did not discover or rediscover reason, but it emancipated it (in a subjectivist sense), and it conferred upon it a dominant and exclusive authority (to the detriment of revelation and tradition), and, finally, it turned it in a new direction. Classical Christian reason was essentially concerned with personal life: reason was supposed to allow each person to master his or her passions and to lead a life in accordance with the nature of a rational animal. Modernity sought to transform reason's perspective; modern reason would focus first on the exterior world; it proposed to change the fate of mankind through the conquest of nature and the mastery of society. The work undertaken by Bacon, Descartes, and Hobbes issued in this revolutionary proposition: to transform the world we must rethink it. Reason was opening up a new era of the human condition.

The modern world thus embarked on a number of great undertakings (scientific, technological, and political), the repercussions of which reason has had to absorb. On the one hand, scientific rationalism (as originally understood) has disqualified itself, giving way to a new version of scientism that considers itself neutral on the subject of "values" and that, as a consequence, emancipates technoscience from all subordination in relation to reason in a higher sense—henceforth reason, committed to transforming things, concerns itself only with means and their efficiency; it is purely instrumental. On the other hand, in the realm of politics, rationalism as an ideology has collapsed, in spite of all the human sacrifices offered to the "Goddess Reason." By contrast, liberal reason has come out the winner and at the same time has been radicalized, cutting its ties, under the influence of equality by default, with nature and with natural ends—henceforth reason as applied to the organization of society is at the service of the diverse and particular objectives that human beings pursue; it is purely procedural.

The result of all these experiences is what we see going on before our eyes: *the growing power of a practical reason cut off from being, a reason reduced to a procedural or instrumental function.* Reason no longer governs in view of ends; it limits itself to determining rules of the game and technical means, all in the service of formal rights and arbitrary goals. In the kingdom of equality by default, reason is ancillary, the reason of specialists; it officially abdicates all civilizing functions. But this is not to say that it abandons the leading role. The techniques forged by the "exact" sciences and the human sciences tend to rule over the whole of human activities. When substantive reason withdraws, technoscientific reason is free to display its whole force. The world, as we have seen, is now considered to be at our disposal; it has no vital distinctions to oppose to the grip of instrumental rationality. Human activities fall back on themselves without any reference points except uncertain and proliferating "human rights." A narrow, specialized, professionalized, technical understanding of reason shapes our world, but without knowing the world it shapes.

To recapitulate: Modern reason (in its contemporary version) has nothing to do with the substantive reason of the Greeks and Christians—it is now taken for granted that there is no "life according to reason." And it is no longer the triumphant modern reason of yesteryear—there is no question of its guiding great material projects associated with the progress of humanity. Rather, reason is now the servant or the master-servant in various external projects, diverse and without compass. It is a servant because it is instrumental to ends it does not govern, and a master-servant in that the economy and technology reign and develop according to their own logic within a world given over to them. What is called the rationalization of the world, following Max Weber, is a procedural and instrumental rationalization in which reason puts itself in the service of the irrational.

2

What can be more rational than a McDonald's restaurant, at least if one reasons in economic and technical terms? There everything is thought through, weighed, calculated, recorded, analyzed; nothing is left to chance or to improvisation. The McDonald's system is the fruit of a "doctrine" developed by a person, Ray Kroc, whose entrepreneurial talent is beyond question.[1] Ray Kroc invented nothing; he borrowed the idea and the principles of fast food from the McDonald brothers from whom he bought the business, and he borrowed from others the principle of franchising. But it was he who knew how to organize, how to extend the principles of organization to the last detail in order to achieve maximum efficiency. With this talent he transformed the art of eating into a very successful technique. The great adventure began in 1955, when Ray Kroc opened the first McDonald's (which today has been raised to the status of a museum). McDonald's proliferated in the United States—in 1961 a Hamburger University was established near Chicago—and then began to appear on other continents. In January 1990, a McDonald's was opened in Moscow a stone's throw from famous Pushkin Square; in April 1992, the largest McDonald's in the world opened its doors in Beijing. The hamburger had set out to conquer the world.

The McDonald's system is a triumph of instrumental rationality. Nothing escapes calculations of profit, always subject to refinement: the size of hamburgers, the restaurant's architecture, the number of fries, the speed of service, the arrangement of parking lots, the affability of the personnel, the interior design, the dimensions of the trays. The system offers standardized products, trains standardized employees, and tends to forge standardized consumers (by the rationalization of margins of choice, the uncomfortable seating, the interior colors). This would be the ideal: robots for employees, a Big Mac for everyone, and consumers in uniform.

The McDonald's system is also a triumph of procedural rationality, a rationality appropriate to a market economy. There, as in the supermarket, the pure spirit of the market reigns. Nothing troubles the purely functional, abstract, impersonal relationship between the seller and the buyer. Here every person, whoever he or she may be, is exactly like all the others; he or she is a consumer, nothing but a consumer, entirely a consumer, a consumer from head to toe. McDonald's is universalist; its calling is to embrace the whole world without regard to divisions. Once one passes through its doors, an alchemy takes over and erases whatever distinguishes and separates: the person becomes a consumer and every consumer's money is as good as any other's. This is the wonder of the system: it neutralizes differences and divisions among people, differences in traits of character, as well as social, national, political, religious, or other differences. It makes coexistence and cooperation possible among people who have nothing in common except respect for the same rules of the game. All over the world, in New York, Paris, Istanbul, or Beijing, McDonald's restaurants welcome you in the same way (automatic smile, guaranteed hygiene, industrial food), whether you are of the left or of the right, Turk or Kurd, Chinese apparatchik or dissident, a child or his grandfather, a policeman or a criminal, a racist or an antiracist. McDonald's is the missionary of a new humanity, the builder of a new world, in collaboration with all the other businesses set to conquer the world market and sharing this great cause with a view to the greatest profit. This new world is undifferentiated, destined to unify itself on the basis of uniform consumption—an egalitarian world, except of course for the only distinction that matters (money), a world called to achieve unity by the grace of the market. The political problem par excellence, the problem that arises from differences among human beings, is finally about to be resolved: consumers of all lands, unite over a Big Mac!

3

For the workers, craftsmen, and peasants whom Péguy fervently evokes at the beginning of *L'Argent,* "all was a rhythm and a rite and a ceremony." At McDonald's, everything is just the opposite of a rite and a ceremony. A ceremony is an intense moment that involves our being, a moment that breaks through the uniform flow of time and sets itself apart in a thousand ways (forms, objects, context), a moment in which human beings share strong feelings. A meal at McDonald's, on the other hand, is a weak moment, a featureless act, a purely functional activity. McDonald's is the functional place par excellence. It reduces everything to a function: things, actions, and people.

Let us take a closer look at things. Here is the final outcome (as seen, I remind the American reader, from the French perspective of the author) of this techno-economic rationality taken to perfection, or almost:

1. The act of eating does not constitute any rhythm in the flow of time. The first principle of the enterprise is to break with time as it is ordered by traditional customs, and more fundamentally to break with all ordering of time. The McDonald's formula is made up first of all by these two golden rules: long hours, brief meals. At McDonald's one eats at any hour and on Sunday just as on any other day. Time there is not regulated—a time for each thing, a time for lunch and a time for dinner—but rather is uniform and uni-

formly at our disposal. It is also rationally divisible; thus, the meal must be shortened as much as possible. The time spent "around the table" is not a separate time, a privileged time in social life. It is subjected like all times to the profit motive. McDonald's time is the time of economic rationality, a time unrelated to the rhythms of life.

2. Formalities, or at least certain formalities, are deliberately absent. Norbert Elias saw the fact of eating with utensils as an important step in "the civilizing of mores." At McDonald's we take a step backwards. There one employs neither plate, nor knife, nor fork; one eats with one's fingers, even the fries that leave one's hands greasy. Why complicate what is rationally so effective and what does not burden the consumer with respect for manners? Respect for procedures is sufficient; formalities are costly and irrational.

3. Things are purely functional; they have nothing to do with human sensibilities. Paper cups, plastic boxes, straws—just a lot of objects so meaningless and worthless that one throws them away after utilization. The whole McDonald's universe is made of plastic, cardboard, synthetic materials—and one has the impression that the food is no exception—materials without nobility or warmth, suited to functional man. The view is of the parking lot, the air is conditioned, cleanliness and ugliness rule—everything is in order. A rose or a tulip would be a cause for surprise in this universe.

4. The food, finally, is the product of an industrial technique that abolishes all nuances of taste. Taste must either be educated or degenerate. It is doubtful that taste becomes more refined by consuming cardboard bread, meat that doesn't taste like meat, sauces that smother all they touch, and desserts crammed with sugar.

This rational universe is in perfect harmony with late modernity. At McDonald's, everyone is equal—but by default. The system reduces human beings to very little: an elementary function. Here, people are gathered, they cross paths, but they share nothing, not a feeling, not a way of being valued even in the least for themselves; they stand side by side in mutual indifference. Here, the other is like me—but he is also a stranger.

McDonald's is a true "nowhere," where a life without rules, order, hierarchy, holidays, symbols, or ceremonies is carried out, a life in which one insignificant moment follows another. Here one speaks only of unimportant things, and one maintains only superficial relations. How could one speak of heartfelt things while chewing on a hamburger? How could one recite a poem between two gulps of a Coke? Who would declare his love over a cheeseburger? McDonald's is not made for such things; it is made for the convenience of the pure consumer, for whom eating means nothing but eating.[2]

By "McDonald's" I of course mean more than McDonald's. If it deserves this excessive honor and reproach, this is because it illustrates and foreshadows the world toward which we are heading, a world shaped by procedural and instrumental reason, a world at once perfected and decivilized.

CHAPTER 9
THE PROCEDURAL RATIONALIZATION
OF THE WORLD

The procedural rationalization of social life flows logically from equality by default. If everyone is judge of what is best for him, if no way of life is any better or any worse than any other, then the social order cannot be based on common ideas or feelings. How then is it possible to arrange things in such a way that people who at the extreme share nothing except their equal freedom agree to live in peace and cooperate with one another? As we have seen, the answer elaborated by the Moderns and radicalized in the contemporary period is the following: since we must renounce all agreement on rules of life, it is necessary to agree on certain rules of the game, rules that guarantee respect for the rights of each person and his or her own goals while at the same time making social cooperation possible. In other words, human beings who disagree must agree on the procedures that allow them to live together in disagreement. The ancients had but modest confidence in procedures and systems: in their eyes, much depended on the actors (who must be motivated to virtuous conduct by education and good customs) and circumstances (of which the best possible use must be made, through the virtue of prudence). To the degree that the Moderns abandoned the idea of virtuous conduct, they were led to base everything on formal rules and to establish a world of rights.

Henceforth, the primary, fundamental fact would be that of the formal rights of man and especially his indeterminate freedom. Nothing is natural in itself; everything must be constructed on the basis of this abstract being known as rights-bearing man. The universal solution is proceduralism.

Thus procedural reason has constantly gained ground. On the one hand, customs inherited from the Western tradition have receded or disappeared, and with them rituals, symbols, forms, and manners. On the other hand, formal law has become more and more dominant and tends to prevail as the unique regulator of human relations. This law has nothing in common with the nature of things; it is reducible to formal rules in the service of individual (and group) rights. The more ground rights occupy, the more it is necessary to regulate things in their service, and the more law gains in extent and loses in substance. A new juridical regime is set up that multiplies rules in order somehow to coordinate the various contending rights. Common life is increasingly regulated by law understood procedurally, which is supposed to maintain order in the absence of meaning. The outcome is essentially the following: (1) the political regime tends to be reduced to regulation and politics to the administration of rights; (2) private relations increasingly take on the form of contractual relations; (3) regulations spread and bureaucracy swells. In a word, social order changes in nature: *substantive law and customs retreat, giving way to contract and regulation.*

1

Procedural reason tends to transform the political regime into a system. As a system, liberal democracy defines itself exclusively by rules of the game, rules that allow sovereign individuals to coexist without impinging on each other and to make collective decisions. The regime is nothing more than a mechanism that works all by itself and independently of the quality of political life. Good politics has no need of virtuous men and women. To be sure, its goals have changed. The liberal-democratic state tends to become no more than an agency serving the rights of individuals and groups. Equality by default implies the withering away of politics.[1]

2

In the sphere of individual relations, contract tends to replace custom and law. If no one has any natural or traditional obligations toward anyone else, then private obligations can only originate from a contract, that is to say, from a formalized and rationalized exchange in which both parties have something to gain. As vital distinctions disappear, the realm of contract spreads. Taken to an extreme, everything can become a matter of exchange organized by contract, in which the assent of autonomous wills is sufficient.

This evolution has many facets, since it touches on the whole of human relations. In the first place, it tends to favor the market, which is the first domain to be emancipated. The market economy surely has great virtues long disdained by French intellectuals. For the first time in history, it made it possible for the great majority of human beings (in the West) to escape poverty, misery, and premature death. But this system, however efficient, is valid only as a particular and subordinate sector of human relations. In the contemporary world, the market ceaselessly extends its influence, not only geographically (economic "globalization"), but also temporally (Sundays fall increasingly under the sway of the market) and socially: the market rules more and more in sports, in culture, and in the arts. It all but dominates the powerful machine known as television. Its influence is visible everywhere; the drumbeat of its slogans is inescapable (in North America, advertising extends to politics and even prescription medications). Since exchange is an activity that presupposes the consent of both parties, by what principle can the contractual procedures of the market be limited? If (as in fact happened in California) a woman who can afford it contracts with her Hispanic maid to carry her child to full term, this is a contract just like any other. The market economy no longer serves ends beyond itself; it is no longer one element of the social order. Rather, it tends to dominate as a form of civilization—the civilization of the market.

This triumph of the market is a triumph of procedural reason. What, after all, is the market economy but the rule of procedures? In market relations, there is no need for a substantive agreement among partners—a formal agreement suffices. The market in a certain sense brings men closer together (Montesquieu wrote some famous pages on the pacifying virtues of commerce), but in another sense it leaves them absolutely indifferent to each other.

This contractualization of human relations takes many forms. Established inequalities (between teachers and students, political leaders and citizens) are reduced, as we have seen, to the measure of contractual bonds. The most personal and intimate relations tend to fit the same model. The world of rights is a world stricken with uncertainty: in the absence of all reference to nature, no one any longer knows what it means to be a man or a woman, a father or a mother. In the language of sociology, "rights undermine roles."[2] Relations with others must be constructed on the basis of contract—and the militant proponents of rights push the process forward.[3] In all Western countries, the tendency, to one degree or another, is the same. Thus, the family in the traditional sense (father, mother, children) is increasingly seen as only one particular kind of family among others. Law diversifies; it abandons all substantive conceptions of the family in the name of the freedom of contracting parties. Everyone chooses the legal form that seems most convenient to him. In the name of indeterminate freedom, procedural reason reduces the family, and more generally all institutions considered to be "mediating bodies," to the status of mere contractual associations, just like a group of stockholders or an athletic club.

3

The world of rights-bearers is that of contract. It is also the world of regulation. There are distinctions to be made according to domains and what is at stake. On the one hand, rights set aside certain obligations, those concerning decency, and tend to favor individual autonomy and contractual freedom; on the other, rights create new obligations, obligations to respect rights, which of course implies public protection but also public action, in particular as concerns the enforcement of equality. As new rights proliferate (equality of results among groups, equal rights for children), formal rules tend to multiply in order to favor equality over differences that oppose equality.

Equality by default opens a practically unlimited field to this kind of regulation. The more it progresses, the more natural and substantive differences no longer make a difference, the more law is called upon to take charge of the social world in order to reconstruct it on the basis of legal abstraction and artificial equality. Taken to the limit, this logic yields the following: if there are no longer any natural differences, why not give the right to vote to infants, why not organize and enforce the exercise of free expression in daycare facilities? If differences among behaviors no longer count, then why should exams require respect for proper handwriting, indeed why penalize the lazy, why be selective when all should have the right to graduate? If all groups (defined by age or sex or geographic origin) are alike in every way, why not distribute positions and offices proportionally? We're not there yet, but that is certainly the way the wind is blowing.

What do we find in the actual practice of rights? The politics of late-modern rights develops anarchically because the notion of "human rights" has lost all consistency, leaving ample room for activists. One moment the politics of rights appeals to universal rights, extending them into new areas (the same education for all, new rights for children); the next it invokes particular rights (rights of "ethnic minorities" in the United States, for example, in the name of equality of results or of "multiculturalism"). But the fundamental axis is always the same: the new rights extend the sphere in which natural and substantive differences are legally neutralized. Consider two examples:

1. *The expansion of universal rights to the point that natural differences are negated.* On November 20, 1989, the United Nations unanimously adopted a new convention on the rights of children. This text begins by reaffirming that the child is a minor and that he or she has the right as a child to "special protection"—up to this point there is no assault on childhood. But suddenly the tone changes and we find the child endowed with new rights that he must himself exercise and that the signatory states must guarantee, "the right to express his opinions on all questions of concern to him" (art. 12), "freedom of thought, conscience, and religion," (art. 14-1), and "freedom of association and freedom of public meeting" (art. 15). What is the meaning of this sharp shift in tone? It represents the progress of ideas tending to deny childhood, ideas that tend to plunge childhood into the world of equality by default. "The child is a person," the militants of the new rights of the child ceaselessly proclaim. More exactly: the child is not a child; he is no longer a person in the making who needs to be loved, guided, and protected, but a complete person whose main attribute is that of modern man: freedom, equal for all and thus also for children.

What do these new rights promise? They pave the way for the increased public regulation and control that are needed in order to put them in practice and finally to ensure that parents and teachers behave as they should. It is important that parents and teachers respect these new rights that belong to those they are supposed to raise—which notion, in essence, forces parents and teachers to abandon their educational responsibilities.[4]

2. *The expansion of the rights of groups to the point that natural differences are negated.* The most striking case is no doubt the following: Especially in the United States and to a lesser degree in Europe (feminism being much more powerful in North America), equality between men and women tends to take on a new meaning. It once meant equality of opportunity; more and more it has come to mean equality of results. This shift came about through the following factual judgment: equality of opportunity implies equality of results. In other words, since women are identical in every way to

men, they must be equally represented in all positions and jobs, and every deviation from the statistical mean can only be the effect of discrimination. Such reasoning justified the American policy of affirmative action implemented in the 1970s in favor of women (following "ethnic minorities"), a policy that in practice meant preferential recruitment in universities, government agencies, and many businesses. The same reasoning in Europe leads to demands for statistical parity between men and women, notably in the selection of political candidates. In France, a law to this effect was passed in 1998.

The problem is that this reasoning is valid only if the inequalities in results between the two sexes have one and only one cause: discrimination. Is this always so? In France, girls do better than boys in secondary school. Does this mean we must denounce some discriminatory policy? But boys are better in mathematics—does this mean mathematics is guilty of gender bias? In all the prisons in the world, there are many more men than women. Are these men victims of discrimination? In all Western nations, women live longer than men. Must this be seen as an infringement of equal rights? One dares not imagine what political corrective the state would have to impose in order to remedy such an infringement. The truth is that men and women are first of all alike as human beings and secondarily different as sexed beings. Though the extent of this difference remains in part uncertain, one would have to be blinded by fanaticism to deny it altogether.

The rejection of all discrimination thus does not imply the adoption of the goal of statistical parity. Otherwise, quotas would have to be applied to all kinds of cases, since the fat, the bearded, the young, only children, Bretons—all are unequally represented in various social positions. Must the state get involved?

4

Procedural reason has its virtues—properly understood, it protects freedoms and contributes to prosperity—but its calling is not to govern the whole of human relations. When it claims to do so by virtue of equality by default, it also contributes to the undoing of manners and morals.

In response to the question, "What does economics economize?" Sir Robertson once gave this lapidary and famous reply: "Love." The answer to the question, "What do procedural rights economize?" is also "love." Left to itself, procedural reason devotes itself to organizing the world of "everyone for himself."

In this world, interest-based organizations and the bureaucracy of rights flourish, but institutions decay. The most obvious example is the family. From the moment familial relations become the stuff of contracts, debts, and accounts receivable, family members are distanced from one another. The philosopher Alain expressed this well: in the family, "everything works without a charter. . . . This is because feelings are sustained by a biological commonality. Here there are no rights, and even the claim to rights is harmful. For example, between brothers and sisters following the death of parents, distribution according to legal rights is irritating; it reminds one of happier times when feelings were enough to keep everything in order. Aristotle said that feeling is a friend of giving and an enemy of trading."[5] A family of rights-holders is a lax and fragile family, a family deficient in loving and being loved. The weakest ones, that is, children, are the first victims of such a family.

Children are also, or will become, victims of their new rights. We may pretend that a child is an adult, but he still remains a child. If protections are abandoned, if parents abdicate, if teachers give up, then social influences will replace the old authorities. The way is open for various seducers. To treat the child as an adult, Alain Finkielkraut writes, "to affirm that he is responsible for his actions, that one must take him at his word and take his preferences at face value, is not to respect or to defend him, but to guarantee the impunity of those who manipulate him. . . . [It is] to expose him, defenseless, to all forms of conditioning and greed."[6] In sum, the state paves the way for demagogues and disreputable advertisers attracted by young flesh and then looks the other way. Procedural reason has no love for children.

CHAPTER 10
THE TWO VERSIONS OF
LIBERAL DEMOCRACY

Two versions of equality govern two versions of liberal democracy. The first is a substantive version, founded on the political recognition of a dignity proper to humanity, of a nature common to all, which justifies but also orders equality and liberty. The second is a procedural version: liberal democracy is identified with certain rules of the game that are supposed to allow human beings without any common substance or natural ends to follow their particular objectives. Of course it is the latter version that is favored by the spirit of the age.

1

The liberal-democratic regime is founded on a first principle, that of equality among men. It is this principle that justifies the democratic organization of power. The simple fact of humanity bestows all the attributes of citizenship; no one has a natural right to command another. In the political order human beings are equal, and it follows that the people—the citizens considered collectively—must either exercise power themselves (direct democracy) or elect those who exercise it (representative democracy). The same principle of equality justifies the liberal limitation of power. Human beings as human beings are bearers of certain rights and liberties; they are equal before the law, and these universal rights define the limits of legitimate action by the democratic government. In other words, a political decision grounded in the equal participation of citizens is valid only within the limits set by the equal liberty of individuals or persons. The principle of universal equality plays out in two different directions, one of which limits the extent of the other. The regime is composite. It follows that in a liberal-democratic regime, contrary to the unfortunate formulations of French constitutional law, the people are not sovereign; if they were, the rights of man would be at the mercy of the will of the majority.

Human beings are thus politically equal. On what grounds? According to equality by default, the equality of citizens flows from the equality of their opinions, which in turn flows from the absence of truth—to each his own "truth," and no one can claim access to the Truth itself. Thus, pluralism is regarded as a virtue in itself. On this view the citizen is accorded no specific dignity, no noble calling; his right to vote is justified in the same way as his individual autonomy, that is, by an essentially negative argument. The exercise of political rights is in turn simplified: the citizen is autonomous by nature, and so there is no need to educate him in freedom. His choice has the same value whether it is the work of his reason or his passions—in fact, such a distinction has no meaning, and so constitutional forms need have no regard for it. All that is needed are simple rules of the game.

Political equality understood substantively rests upon an altogether different argument. The equality of citizens is only a convention, but it is the convention that best accords with the fundamental equality of human beings and with the dignity of each human being. The democratic principle put an end to the time when birth put one man above another; it gave a voice to the humble, the obscure, the common man, and limited the pretensions of the great and the pride of the refined. Men in power are tempted to take themselves for beings of another species and to look down on ordinary people. Democratic equality (in its substantive version) goes against this natural tendency; it embodies an essential similarity that trumps all claims to superiority, in particular institutionalized superiority. It likewise recognizes in every individual the quality of a reasoning creature, a being capable of choice and concern for the common good. In this way—and here is its fundamental virtue—it gives honor to every human being and in particular to ordinary people.

It follows that the act of voting is surrounded by the solemnity appropriate to a judicial act, and that it must be prepared and managed in such a way as to cause reason and the common good to prevail as much as possible over passion and particular interests. The citizen must be educated to the exercise of his rights (civic education), and these rights must be exercised according to defined formalities (scheduling of elections, deliberative procedures, etc.). The will of the people must not be confused with a momentary whim, nor liberal democracy with mere procedures.

2

In the world of equality by default, each individual is the judge of his own good, and it is impossible to be mistaken. It follows that politics no longer has anything to do with the purposes of life or the best way of life. From this point of view, liberal democracy is nothing but a legal category; it is defined exclusively by two fundamental rules. The first is the *liberal rule* (formalist version), the point of which is to neutralize disagreements concerning ways of life. It expresses itself as follows: these issues have nothing at all to do with politics but rather are purely a matter of the sovereign choices of individuals. The state claims to be neutral and agnostic before different "values" or "lifestyles," and an impermeable barrier separates the public and the private. Politics is secular in a radical sense; it is indifferent to all questions of manners and morals.

The second rule applies in the political arena. Here of course we have in mind the *democratic rule,* which institutionalizes disagreements and establishes a procedure of arbitration: universal suffrage and majority rule. Considered formally, this rule is in itself sufficient. Democracy is a machine that is in working order as long as everyone respects the rules of the game. The qualities of the participants matter little, for the system sees to everything.

The substantive version of liberal democracy does not deny these rules of the game—the regime has by nature a procedural dimension—but it interprets them differently. The scope of each of these two rules is interpreted differently, and so, especially, is the scope of the procedures themselves. The essential point is this: *the rules of the game are not sufficient.* They are not sufficient to forge a true political society, nor to make a liberal-democratic regime a good regime. No system suffices by itself, and much depends on the conduct of participants. Procedural politics founded on equality by default benefits from the appeal of simple ideas, but it ignores a number of essential (or substantial) distinctions: the distinctions between a "society" and a "community," between a corrupt and a healthy people, between a demagogue and a statesman, passion and reason, procedures and forms. . . . Emptied of substance, political society falls apart.

This fundamental distinction can be developed in a series of secondary distinctions that concern all aspects of the regime. For example:

1. *The social bond.* The procedural version of liberal democracy tends to reduce society to a conglomerate of individuals who agree only on respecting the rules. But does an agreement on the rules of the game suffice to make a strong society? Who would risk his life to defend procedures, either those of the political regime or those of the market? And can this agreement itself be solid if the members of the society have nothing in common? According to the substantive version, political society cannot be reduced to a mere association. The liberal-democratic regime is itself founded on certain "values," those implied by substantive equality; moreover, this regime cannot be established successfully except in a community forged in the

modern era, that is, a nation. Liberal democracy and the nation-state can only be separated at great risk.

Why this bond? Liberal democracy is by nature hostile to nationalism (since it is based on a universalism rejected by the nationalist spirit), but it cannot afford to dispense with the particular bonds created by membership in a nation. For the foreseeable future, the bonds of community must be particular bonds, and the very character of a regime requires such bonds. The essential reason for this fact is that liberal democracy privileges discord and establishes majority rule as the principle of decision making in the political sphere. In order to sustain this institutionalization of conflict, there must be a strong sense of common belonging. There are costs inherent in this regime, prices to pay; the regime requires, in particular, that when minorities are overruled they recognize the legitimacy of decisions made by the representatives of their adversaries. This cost is bearable and is borne in Western regimes for two reasons: (1) because these democratic regimes are also liberal (and the liberal rule limits the scope and cost of the democratic rule); and (2) because of the existence of communitarian bonds forged by national unity. There are of course counterexamples: Canada and Belgium, which are divided into two communities and which tinker and feel their way toward viable solutions; and a number of African states in which tribal rivalries and the absence of a true nation are major obstacles to the establishment of, and respect for, liberal-democratic rules.

If this analysis is correct, liberal democracy requires a substance external to itself: a common memory, shared references, awareness of a common destiny. In this sense, to wish to go beyond the nation and, as Jürgen Habermas proposes, forge a post-national Europe on the basis of a "constitutional (that is, procedural) patriotism" is to advocate weak citizenship and a political society without substance; it is also to risk undermining the foundations of liberal democracy.

2. *Political obligations.* When liberal democracy is considered to be a machine, respect for procedures is supposed to suffice, and cit-

izens and leaders are relieved of all other obligations—the system can do without the civic virtue of its participants. Yet the rules of the game cannot themselves function in the complete absence of feelings of civic obligation: the outcome of an election never comes down to one person's vote, and so the citizen, if he were purely selfish and rational, would never vote because he knows that his vote will not change the outcome at the polls. Moreover, respect for formal rules in no way guarantees good government: is it a matter of indifference whether the officeholder is an honest man or a scoundrel, a statesman or a demagogue? The good functioning of the regime depends upon a shared sense of responsibility concerning the common destiny.

This necessity becomes plainly apparent in extreme situations. In wartime, if individual aims prevail over the common interest, then what becomes of the country's defense? Extreme situations remind us that politics is not just one activity among others and that the common interest can go so far as to require that men risk their lives. But if the sense of political obligation weakens or even disappears in ordinary times, what strength will it have in those dramatic moments when much more is expected? Procedural democracy navigates well enough in calm waters, but it may become vulnerable when the wind begins to blow. During the time when the United States was committing itself to the First World War, the recruitment posters showed Uncle Sam, wearing a severe expression and pointing his finger, with only these words: "I want you." On the eve of the Gulf War of 1990, the army's recruiting slogan had a very different tone: "Be all that you can be in the army." More recently, the slogan has become "an army of one." The seduction of "self-expression" has replaced the discourse of civic responsibility.[1] Does this bode well for political cohesion?

3. *Forms.* Procedural democracy is limited to procedures, whereas substantive democracy is regulated by forms. Procedures are neutral and empty; they are expressions of juridical abstraction. Forms, on the other hand, whether embodied in morals and manners or in law,

contain meaning; they have the effect not only of regulating but also of elevating human action.

Consider a day of legislative elections in the year 2028: the voting age has been lowered to sixteen years of age (or—why not?—fourteen); terms have been reduced to one year (or six months); the office of representative has no prestige (an elected official is considered by voters to be a mere delegate, an agent in the service of their desires and interests); political debate is without rules and takes the form of advertising slogans and personal attacks; indeed, the very idea of rational debate has vanished (for what is there to discuss if all arguments are equal because all are equally devoid of rationality?); passions are expressed crudely, and many, especially the youth, treat elections very casually or with indifference. In short, democratic choice has become a circus, yet the procedural rules are intact (but for how long?). Everything is just fine in the world of procedures.

But now consider another election in some remote corner of the world: the term of office is reasonably long, the voting age is sensible, the office of representative is viewed as honorable, and those chosen are first of all the most capable and the most worthy; political debate is moderate; sufficient time is allowed for a real exchange of ideas and for the presentation of well-argued speeches; the act of voting is imbued with solemnity, and citizens have the sense of engaging in something important—they are aware of their great responsibility. The election appeals to what is highest in them, and the appropriate formalities contribute to this sense of elevation.

This contrast is no doubt somewhat strained, but it serves to illustrate the insufficiency of mere procedures and the virtue of forms (provided these do not become sterile). Such forms may be embodied either in usages and customs or in legal, and especially constitutional, rules. Thus, constitutional interpretation differs according to the different versions of the regime: whereas, in one case, the constitution is nothing but a juridical framework, an institutional mechanism, in the other it is much more, a subtle ordering of legal rules in order to motivate participants to act in a way that favors the proper functioning of the regime, which is to say that it speaks the language of forms. The best example that one can give of such a use of forms is doubtless that of the American Constitution.[2] The Founding Fathers intended to establish a "popular" or democratic regime, but also a good government. How was this to be done? Madison, Hamilton, and the other framers of the Constitution were pioneers with the wisdom to design institutional forms in the service of two objectives: on the one hand, to moderate and temper "popular government"; on the other, to ennoble the practice of democracy. On the one hand, to avoid all abuse of power (in causing ambition to counter ambition within a system of checks and balances); on the other, to reinforce the reason of the people and the civic virtue of their leaders by a system of delegation, incentives, and roles (the effect of representation and the distance between the people and power, as well as the design of public offices in order to create a "tendency to responsible government").

The Constitution of 1787 has been a remarkable success in that it still governs American political life, but the procedural interpretation that now prevails no longer allows institutional forms to play the role of elevating political life. Government is considered more and more to be a mere delegated agent rather than a set of responsible institutions working within a space conducive to deliberation and judgment and aiming at the rational consent of the people. Representation is now hardly more than a technical necessity, not a means of increasing the role of reason. The procedural version of democracy devalues representation and deliberation, leaving the field open to informal practices that in turn contribute to the decline of constitutional forms.

What are these informal practices? In the United States, France, and elsewhere, they are above all the result of the influential role of opinion polls and the media. Opinion polls (a product of the social sciences) and the information machine (especially television) come together to undermine the role of representation and deliberation.

Polls tend to pervert the relationship between voters and elected officials. Rather than asking who is worthy of holding public office and to what ends, as is the case with elections (properly understood), they invite citizens to believe that their current opinions and attitudes must be immediately adopted by the government. Polls have no respect for the timing of elections; they press for immediate results, measured by ratings, which are in turn determined by other polls. Everything comes down to statistics established by experts and transmitted by the media. The work of politicians is thus altered, and citizens learn nothing important by knowing how many of their fellow citizens share their opinion on a given question. How can such a figure help them to exercise better judgment?[3]

The rule of immediacy owes still more to the media. Television "short-circuits" representative institutions; it delivers "news" directly to the public at a frenetic pace and solicits immediate reactions. Politicians are expected to announce their decisions almost instantaneously; they have time neither to reflect nor to deliberate, and their immediate reaction itself feeds the flow of news. The public is interrogated by pollsters without any more prior deliberation, and its reaction is likely to elicit further immediate reactions. The information machine implicitly requires that the government be ready at every moment to respond to the demands of "public opinion," more or less filtered through the media. Officeholders are relieved of all pedagogical functions, since citizens are supposed to possess all the means for deciding immediately for themselves on the basis of information provided above all by television. The decline of forms leaves the field open to a "democracy of opinion" that is vulnerable to foul play. Without democratic forms, "voice" is generally a weapon of the strong.

3

There is no such thing as a perfect solution where the organization of political or social life is concerned. Liberal democracy, in its substantive version, is a composite regime. It does its best to combine several principles. Its perpetual challenge is to search out points of equilibrium: between authority and liberty, rights and moral customs, the aims of individuals and the interest of the community, private and public, communitarian and contractual bonds, procedures and substance. But when procedural reason overwhelms everything else, the equilibrium is destroyed—liberalism pushed to the point of relativism occupies practically the whole ground, and so it denatures and devalues democratic choice. At the end of the day, *politics withers away;* it is stripped of its specific purposes. If only separate individuals matter, individuals with nothing in common but their individual freedom, then to what can one appeal in order to account for a common interest beyond particular interests? Politics arbitrates one way or another between interests and rights, but it renounces all responsibility as far as civilization is concerned. As a result, the collective destiny is excluded from all deliberation and all rational choice; it is cobbled together haphazardly, the mere result of a myriad of dispersed preferences. The abdication of democratic politics means that human beings have renounced all control over their common destiny, that they have abandoned it to the logic of rights and to the logic of the market and technical reason. When procedural reason rules, the field is wide open to instrumental reason.

CHAPTER 11
THE INSTRUMENTAL RATIONALIZATION OF THE WORLD

1

Late modernity is a blessed age for the children of Prometheus. On the one hand, it emancipates them all but completely; on the other, it puts means of unprecedented power in their hands. Reason tends to be stripped of all jurisdiction over human activities (except as understood procedurally in terms of formal rights); it follows that activities directed toward the conquest of nature are liberated from all subordination and all limitations: everything is feasible, everything is manipulable, everything is fit to be seen by everyone. Modern reason abdicates in the order of ends; at the same time, it arms human action with all the power of the applied sciences. Henceforth, practical reason is identified with a technoscientific knowledge (specialized, formalized, and impersonal know-how) produced by scientific research (whether in the natural or human sciences). Scientific tools are free to develop autonomously.

What is at stake here must not be underestimated. Scientific techniques are not of the same nature as traditional techniques. The latter belong to the world of human experience; they take the form of tools that extend the activity of the body. The former belong to another world, a separate world, that of science—a world that, as we have seen, is cut off or remote from human experience. Technoscientific man presents himself as external to a world that he looks at through the lenses of science and views as being at his disposal. As a result, modern techniques take the form of machines or processes governed by pure efficiency, independently of all other considerations: "Whatever one can do, one does; what is important is what works—as understood, of course, from my point of view as a specialist; the rest is of no concern to me." *The world is given over to a knowledge severed from life and unburdened of all responsibility.* Rationality is purely instrumental.

Instrumental reason is this utilitarian reason, a reason confined to the realm of having, which is preoccupied with the efficiency of means in the service of an end that it does not question. It advances blindly, governed by a single principle: more is better. Henceforth, the way is open; it has the formidable means of scientific techniques at its disposal, and so it can work in conditions that are in a sense pure and perfect in the service of the imperative of having more and more: more speed, more merchandise, more firepower, more performance, more machines, news, energy, comfort, images, orgasms, records, and so on. But is it all really worth the trouble? What becomes of all that escapes scientific means, of what human beings experience, feel, and live? Such questions are irrelevant. Instrumental rationality is that of the information technology expert who sees in computer horoscopes or computer sex nothing but technical progress; that of the journalist who mobilizes huge technical resources in order to save a few minutes or a few seconds in transmitting the news; that of the engineer who assesses his work in terms of the amount of concrete he lays over the earth; that of the doctor who treats human sexuality like machinery; that of the businessman who judges artists and athletes by their commercial value; that of the biologist for whom artificial procreation is just one form of biological manipulation among many others, and so forth. In each case, the question is considered in technical terms and the objective is to have ever more. Instrumental rationality is indifferent to the substance of life; it transforms the way people live without raising the question of ways of life (except perhaps superficially). The children of Prometheus no longer know what a man of flesh and bones is, and they laugh at the anger of the gods.

Let me be clear that what is in question here is of course not all forms of technical rationality—no one can be a good architect, or sculptor, or historian, without technical proficiency—nor every form of technoscientific rationality—who would repudiate the victories won against disease, the easing of physical labor, the near elimination of material misery, Mozart on a compact disc or Molière in paperback? What is in question here is technoscientific rationality left to its own devices, that is, its logic taken as a whole. One might say that technoscience operates behind a mask; it contradicts itself but plays upon this contradiction. It wants to be neutral and it wants to be autonomous. In other words, it claims to have nothing to do with "values," and at the same time it claims to escape all subordination. But one of two things must be true: either technoscience is neutral and it cannot govern itself (with reference to what?), or it governs itself and so it is not neutral (it pursues certain goals). In practice, the claim of neutrality has the effect of relieving technoscience of all questioning concerning the meaning of its activity. A fictitious neutrality justifies a blind autonomy. Technoscience works in the dark but forbids anyone to guide it (thanks to scientism, no one has a lantern).

Obviously my theme here is not original. Criticisms and warnings concerning technoscience have not been lacking from the pens of philosophers and writers (Péguy, Gabriel Marcel, Martin Heidegger, Jacques Ellul, Michel Henry). But the technicians are none the wiser; they rush forward, each on his own track.

2

There is no need to dwell on the growing power of instrumental rationality, since it is everywhere evident—in the landscape that surrounds us, in professional life, in daily existence. Activities are becoming more and more specialized and technical, each one developing in its own domain according to its own logic. Without anyone overseeing the campaign, instrumental rationality advances on all fronts. It advances in various forms, and especially these two: techno-technical rationality (technique for the sake of technique), and techno-economic rationality (technique in the service of economic utilitarianism)—two sometimes competing but often complicit and even interwoven forms of rationality that always tend in the same direction.[1]

What is this direction? The world they make is a comfortable world wherein material life is gentler and ancestral forms of servitude fade away; but it is also a world wherein life shrinks. Instrumental reason is in tune with equality by default; it is liberated from all that is given by nature. It never considers man to be a composite being, a whole that can only be dissociated artificially; it never looks at nature as a vital domain. It treats man as if he were made up of separate functions and treats nature as an object of conquest and manipulation; finally man himself is treated like an object of mastery and manipulation. This instrumental mentality changes one's relation to the world—the more ground it gains, the more widespread is the metamorphosis to which it subjects human beings. Taken to an extreme, each person becomes both an agent and an object of technique.

1. *Functional man.* Instrumental reason is set in motion by fractions of human beings who consider only fractions of human beings. The world becomes peopled by human fractions, human functions. Whether as an agent or an object of the process of rationalization, whether as a specialist or an object of a specialty, the subject disintegrates.

And so it goes in activities of production. Techno-economic rationality promotes the division and the specialization of activities; it brushes aside practical knowledge (the artisan's intuitive know-how, personal and informal knowledge) in favor of impersonal and technical knowledge.[2] There is nothing new in this account, but the process has accelerated since the days of Marx and Spengler. This doubtless increases productivity, but does the resulting cost for the human worker count for nothing? What is true for the human producer is also or tends to become true for the human consumer. Rationality requires that the activities of consumption become increasingly specialized, increasingly limited to a single function. A place for each thing: a place for shopping that is designed only for shopping (supermarkets), a place for eating where one goes only to eat (McDonald's and its imitators), a place for fun that is rationally organized for this purpose (Disneyland, vacation clubs, Las Vegas), and of course a place that juxtaposes almost all these functional activities, the shopping mall. Everything is rationalized for the satisfaction of the consumer. The arrangement is obviously very efficient. But the other side of the story is that man is not merely a consuming animal.

This fragmentation of man has many other facets. Instrumental logic has led or is leading to this: What is a champion athlete? Not a person devoted to and excelling in a sport, but a record-making machine that must be prepared for this outcome, and also a commercial asset, a human function straining toward his unique goal, which is determined by his function. You ask about the spirit of sportsmanship? That might have had a place in the day of amateurs. Today, champions are professionals and specialists: nothing counts but the result.

What is a sick person? Not a human being with an illness but an affected organ, a function in disrepair. Instrumental medicine is a technique of repair, extremely specialized and very effective as far as it goes—but for the rest, go see another specialist. A sick person might also be a number taken from a cost-benefit analysis that indicates the worth of his life. "What do you think of the theory according to which human life is priceless?" someone once asked an American economist? The response deserves to be immortalized: "We have no data to this effect."[3]

What is a poor person? Not someone who is poor for such and such a reason and who experiences poverty in such and such a way, but a poor person pure and simple as defined by his income and only by that. The human being disappears behind a statistical abstraction constructed by the social sciences. One has only to drive through a black ghetto in the United States to see the result: a human wasteland.

What is a politician? A specialist in management? A porn star? Just another kind of specialist, very gifted in his specialty. No activity engages the whole being, sex no more than any other. It is separated from the rest and derives from an autonomous technique. What, finally, is life? A collection of separate activities, each governed by its own technique; a series of distinct problems, each with its own technical solution. The human function need not worry; he has methods for practically everything: for making friends, for loving himself, for overcoming depression, for eating without getting fat, for succeeding without effort, for always achieving orgasm, for learning a language in a couple of weeks, for getting along with his boss, for cheating on his wife without feeling guilty. I exaggerate only slightly: books of this kind take up entire shelves in American bookstores. Instrumental reason is within everyone's reach: upon the ruins of meaning flourish the techniques of "having more."

2. *Nature as object and the grip of the technical world.* Instrumental reason sees in human nature nothing but matter at its disposal, matter delivered over to the human will; instrumental reason strips human life of all intrinsic value. Technoscientific man does not take part as a human being in what he does; he objectifies the world to use it or enjoy it without loving it (Gabriel Marcel). His aim is not to cooperate with nature, to "command it by obeying it," but to exploit it as much as possible: what matters is what can be made useful. For the functional man, the earth is conquered territory. Yet a real human being is not a stranger in this world; an ordinary man is attuned to the world of the senses (he appreciates the beauty of a place and the savor of a piece of fruit), and even the scientist is attuned to the intelligible world (there are mathematical truths nature knows without ever having learned them). Still techno-

science remains blind to the bonds between man and nature; it makes no distinctions—except in terms of utility, profit, and efficiency—between wood and plastic, stone and concrete, bread and a pill, a house integrated with a countryside and a high-rise that disfigures it, a city and a sprawling development.[4] Nature is exploitable and malleable at will. If there is any feeling foreign to the instrumental mentality, it is indeed that of respect.

But just how are transgressions to be defined? As is often the case, the difficulty consists in finding the point of equilibrium. When technoscience takes non-human nature as its object, it proceeds as if man had no anchoring in nature. Deep ecology succumbs to the opposite excess when it dissolves man in nature and denies what makes him a distinct being, that is, denies that he is a being who transcends his biological nature.[5] Nature is not a mother—she cannot be more than a mother-in-law, as Chesterton says—but neither is she our slave, and when we consider her as a slave, we do violence to ourselves.

How does the progress of instrumental reason reveal itself in practice? Nature, reduced to an object, disappears as a vital sphere. Technoscience replaces a natural sphere cared for by human beings with a completely different sphere, one that is artificial and uniform and has nothing to say to human feelings. The functional sites that multiply in our societies and indeed metastasize to the four corners of the planet are "non-places" (Marc Auge), places without soul, cold and impersonal. Today, to take a long trip involving a number of flights is to find oneself in what seems an interminable hallway. Airports as well as shopping centers, "international" hotels, modern train stations, university campuses, buildings (whether constructed as high-rises or in the style of fortifications) are all built on the same pattern: they are made for the satisfaction of the human function (and of the egos of architects and urban planners). They are without substance, places without history, without beauty (with a few exceptions), without any symbolic dimension. One can become attached to a piece of land, a house, a belltower, a city; but who can experience any strong feeling in these spaces that express the power of modern technology? All is functionalized, even time, which is cut off from natural rhythms. In the cities composed of large, sterile building complexes in North America, there is no more evening, no more morning, no more spring, and no more winter. Time is homogeneous and uniform; it is the time of technique. The creature distances himself from the Creation.

The creature also distances himself from his fellow beings. "Nonplaces" isolate people who have nothing to share and who form only a "lonely crowd." The techniques of diversion lead to the cultivation of what one might call solitary pleasures (video games, Walkmans, slot machines, television). In the end, the techniques of "communication" come between human beings. Here modern man leaps up in amazement: "How can you talk that way? Your hostility to technology leads you astray. Our day is, on the contrary, that of communication. Every individual can enter into almost instantaneous contact with the world, thanks to the wonders of technology. I'm never without my cell phone; I am connected directly with many databases; I send and receive instant messages thanks to the Internet; I get fifty television channels and I'm up to date immediately on everything. And you try to tell me I'm cut off from others? Come now, you're losing it; never have people been so close to each other." "Then allow me to ask you this question: how do you 'communicate' with your wife and your children, by fax or by computer?" "Don't confuse matters. Anyway, my wife left me. And my personal problems are none of your business."

Without question the means of modern communication have certain utilitarian virtues, but they hardly, or at least imperfectly, lend themselves to the kind of exchanges that matter, and by relying on them excessively the spirit shrivels. Technology is not neutral: the means influence (more or less) the content. Is it possible to imagine Seneca teaching wisdom to Lucilius by Internet, Heloise and Abelard exchanging faxes, or Pascal writing his *Memorial* on a word processor? All that has to do with technical knowledge, especially mere information, can easily be transmitted electronically, but this is in general much less true for anything of vital significance, anything that engages our being. Of course one must make certain distinctions: not all technologies are impersonal to the same degree; some may serve as a respectable second best, and the way they are used makes a difference. But what interests us here is a general tendency, one that does not bring human beings together. True communication implies the collaboration of feelings, a personal relation, in a word, an encounter—whether such an encounter involves flesh and blood contact, a book, a work of art, or a theatrical play. Encounters are those blessed moments when one human being finds himself in tune with another or with the work of another, and thus finds access to being. But when the machine comes on the scene, it creates many parasites. It creates by its very nature a certain distance. It imposes certain requirements such as those of speed. Finally and above all, it is a machine, an increasingly advanced machine that raises its user to the level of a master of technique; in this way it flatters his ego but does little to foster openness. A genuine encounter requires time, availability, self-effacement—all things not fostered by the use of communication devices. On the contrary, excessive use of these technologies leads to a muffling of sensibilities. Consider a young man who from a very young age is bombarded with images, computer programs, e-mail exchanges, synthetic music—what can he share with another, except brutal sensations and at most cold ideas? In the world to come, people will be equipped with a thousand means for communicating at every moment at any distance, but will they have anything to say that matters?

3. *The human object.* In the final stage of the conquest of nature, man's biological being is itself called to become an object of mastery and manipulation. A wholly homogeneous world is a wholly available world: man belongs to this formless, undifferentiated, malleable nature, now offered up to his own power. Or, more precisely, man as agent of technoscience, who situates himself as it were out-

side nature, sees in man as object of technoscience only one natural object like any other. Technoscientific man looks down on his fellows, but he cannot account for his own power, a power that distinguishes humanity from the rest of nature—except by taking himself to be an exception.

However that may be, technoscience reduces the human body to a mere organism. As a result, the different parts of the body are understood solely according to biological criteria (there is no difference except in degree between a bone, a nerve, and the gametes), and reproduction becomes just one organic function among others. And now we see that progress in biology is opening up the field of reproduction to dizzying possibilities of human intervention. The technologies of artificial reproduction do not only offer ways to fight sterility (by splitting up the act of procreation into component parts); they also make it possible, eventually, to select and program the child who is to be born. What is emerging is the power to determine, in collaboration with technicians, what kind of child one will create. At the collective level, this amounts to the power to control the evolution of the species. If this comes to pass, certain human beings will have a truly unprecedented power over others (future generations). Technology is playing with fire.

Here instrumental logic meets the logic of rights. (Technoscientific man and rights-bearing man are of course on the same side.) The "right to a child" invoked to justify recourse to scientific techniques opens the door to any practice found to be technologically possible. This right to a child has a childish desire at its foundation; and if desire is the ground of rights, then the right to a child is not only indifferent to context, it can legitimately become the right to such-and-such a child endowed with specific characteristics. If I want to program my child, for what reason could anyone refuse me this right, which technology makes possible? The very principles of late modernity are at stake in this question. The alternative is clear: either there is a natural order, in this case the order of procreation (in which the child has his own standing), and individual desire is no more sovereign than technology is autonomous; or there is no binding natural order and one person's "I can" needs no more justification than another person's "I want." In this case nothing is in principle excluded: a woman who carries her daughter's child, a child born from a father long dead, a mother the age of a grandmother, a child who is the twin of his father, human embryos given up to experimentation, a child accepted or rejected according to certain specifications and aptitudes, a child made to order and delivered with a guarantee . . .

Confronted with this dilemma, our societies have generally chosen half measures. On the one hand, legislators have been called to come to the rescue in order to set limits on new technologies. How, after all, can one simply give science a green light? No doubt it has never been clearer that instrumental reason cannot be left to its own devices nor society abandoned to the anarchy of individual desires (even when converted into rights); in other words, the dangers of irresponsible freedom have never been so evident. And yet, on the other hand, the resulting legislation does not measure up to the challenge; it takes more or less the form of tinkering (and sometimes avoids the issue), and it is doubtful that such legislation will be enough to stem the tide of biotechnology. Politics refuses to give any substantial content to the idea of human nature, and so the dikes that it builds have no foundation but sand and are weakened by numerous cracks. What we see emerging most clearly is a child of a new kind, a child who will be the result of prior choices (from among a larger and larger menu of options), a child made to order.

This child will be, in other words, a child whose parents will have decided how he must be—no longer a unique being received in wonder amidst the mystery of life, but a child selected or made to order thanks to technology, not the fruit of an unconditional commitment, but a being subject to certain conditions. Such a child will be a child subject to reservations, deprived of the freedom to be what he is, a child who will know that he is there only because he met certain requirements—a second-rate child.

3

The nefarious consequences of instrumental rationalization are of two orders. Some leap out at us; they affect our external lives and biological natures and give rise to worries and reactions: the nuclear threat, pollution, the waste of limited resources, chaotic urbanization, the economic division of the world, the threat of eugenics. These are problems politics cannot ignore, though the response often appears quite timid in the face of an instrumental reason intoxicated with its power and determined to pursue its mad course.

And then there are the hardly visible consequences, those of which we have spoken, which touch the substance of our lives. The end—that is, civilization—is lost from view, and the means—modern science—"barbarizes" us (Nietzsche). In the world that instrumental reason is now creating in collaboration with procedural reason, those who experience ordinary human feelings will feel like strangers. Experts, specialists, and professionals will have given birth to a world in which they will only meet others like them. But it would be unjust to cast stones: they know not what they do.

CHAPTER 12
THE WORLD AS MEANINGLESS SPECTACLE

1

Last night or the day before, a reporter on the television news announced that the dollar had gained or had lost two or three points against the euro or the yen. What are we to make of this? Is a variation of a few points significant? How is it to be explained? What are its effects? In a word, what is the meaning of this information? I confess my ignorance, but I am doubtless in good company. Indeed, it is doubtful whether the reporter himself is in a better position. In other words, it is likely that the information has no meaning either for the giver or the receiver. And yet, to judge by the reporter's expression, this is no game. Look at him: he's not kidding. His seriousness and conviction are reassuring. He looks straight ahead at his TelePrompTer, and his delivery is flawless. He is a true "professional"—he does not know what he is saying, but he says it well.

Of course this meaninglessness is not without significance. It reflects an interpretation of what we need to know and what it takes to know something, the same interpretation on which the whole operation of the gigantic information machine, including both images and words, is based. This epistemology remains ever implicit—the machine avoids any self-questioning—but there is no mystery in it. Essentially it consists of the following propositions:

1. *The meaning of raw information is immediately accessible to everyone.* The latest trend on the financial exchanges is of course not a pure piece of information (it is constructed and selected), but it is raw information in the sense that it is given without explanation. Even the specialist can offer no more than conjectures concerning the reasons for the day's result. And does he even know whether the subject in which he is a specialist is important or meaningful for human life?

Note, too, that the speech in question is addressed to everyone. Plato said that speech is preferable to writing because it can be adapted to its addressee. The electronic word does not have this advantage, but it hardly cares, since its monologue aims at all audiences. The idea that knowledge involves distinct levels and stages is foreign to the machine—in this sense, television is an enemy of true pedagogy.

The content of broadcast news is essentially raw information. To be sure there is some commentary, but this is always brief—events won't wait—and generally very closely related to a particular story. On the American television networks, the average time devoted to each subject in a news program is less than a minute. The implicit assumption is that what's going on in the world is immediately intelligible, that the facts, the data, the images practically speak for themselves. Technology allows us to be present everywhere (at least as far as is allowed politically), to exist in immediate contact with every event or pseudo-event. Satellites and computers, microphones and cameras, all these extraordinary means come together to deliver the world to us—how could we doubt that they provide us with every key to understanding? With supreme confidence, technology offers us direct access to knowledge.

Consider the attitude of a television reporter: He has the air of an expert, confident manners, a dry and rapid delivery. Everything in his demeanor says, "You can trust me; reality is as I say, and not otherwise." Who ever heard a journalist admit, "Civil war has arisen again in a faraway land. Why? I have no idea, and I really don't care." Or, "The European monetary system is not working. Just what does that mean? Don't ask me." And we are no more likely to hear, "The meaning of this conflict is hard to grasp; the significance of that statement is quite elusive. . . ." To say "I do not know" is forbidden in broadcasting by "professional" standards.

Thus, in this gigantic enterprise called "communication," there is a more or less conscious element of fakery—on the part of the speakers and, probably, the listeners. The listener is invited to believe that he understands or at least to pretend that he understands. The postulate of immediate intelligibility benefits from an intimidation effect, that powerful injunction not to say, "I do not understand."

2. *Only the present, especially the immediate present, is important.* How is it possible to sleep in peace without knowing the latest fluctuations of the dollar? Nietzsche recommended a cushion of three centuries between one's age and oneself; today radios and televisions cause us to live the age day by day, hour by hour, even minute by minute. To know means to know immediately what is happening; not a minute must be lost before spreading the news. During elections, television networks compete with each other to be the first to announce the result. In 1988, CBS beat out the competition: it announced the victory of George Bush two minutes ahead of the rest. That's two minutes, one hundred twenty seconds, gained in announcing the outcome—what a success, what progress in knowledge! Surely these seconds are well worth the millions of dollars they cost; after all, those who spent this money are serious people. And one cannot consider without sadness those who went to sleep, or to reflect, or to pray at that moment, those who had to wait until the next day to know—they must be tormented with remorse!

Thus the present moment is everything, and a mood of urgency prevails. "For the French government (which shares this privilege with the Church), the long term means eternity. For the present government, the long term is a six-month period. For the press, the long term is a day. For television, the long term is an instant."[1] And so the news of one instant crowds out the news of the previous instant. From one day to the next, a subject or a person goes from the light of day to darkness; time is reduced to an instant, and the instant is scattered into a flurry of information in which the serious and the trivial, the tragic and the ridiculous are jumbled: a Sikh or Tamil revolt, the fall of the dollar and the Lakers' margin of victory, the rise of the dollar and of the president's popularity, ten deaths in some attack and three goals for Marseille . . .

This media-time, a time completely fragmented, discontinuous, and without memory, this dislocated time swallows up and flattens everything. If the machine happens to report something important, it reduces it to its own measure. It imposes a brevity that excludes nuance, development, and in-depth reflection. The machine is not neutral as regards ideas; it works to the benefit of simple and cold ideas, those which technology is suited to convey. The expert is more at ease before the camera than is the poet. And even if someone manages to say something important, it is immediately thrown into the impetuous and confused flux of news, at the same level as every unimportant thing. The machine never stops running. It grinds ceaselessly, indeed it keeps on accelerating and is proud of it. Nothing matters enough to cause the machine to stop or take a break. The machine belongs to the world of technology; there it follows its natural course, that of instrumental reason: more is better. There is no such thing as too much news; the race is never fast enough—with a little more effort we can make our world a little more ephemeral, a little more fleeting.

3. *Image is everything.* What matters in the world is especially what the cameras show. The logic of technology dictates the following: what is seen is more important than what cannot be filmed, so what can be filmed must be filmed in every case. In other words, what counts is what can be shown, and there is practically nothing that cannot be shown.

This technical criterion is of course not the only one, but it is a major factor in deciding what subjects will be treated and how much time will be devoted to them. The importance of an event derives from the presence of cameras and the visual power of the available images. From this point of view, the exchange rate is no doubt pretty poor material, even if presented in graphic form. Much more interesting are all the spectacular images of which the machine is so fond. In this sense catastrophe is a boon, and all the more so a catastrophe that can be filmed close-up. For the same reason, a beating recorded on film is more important than thousands of deaths unseen by the electronic eye. The image has its own worth; it is as autonomous as all techniques in the world of equality by default. Left to itself, the machine has no criterion for distinguishing what may be shown from what must not be shown. Its logic is to show everything: the agony of a little Colombian girl dying in 1985, a pile of corpses, brutal violence in action. The camera looks on with a cold eye; it transforms into a spectacle what civilization once covered with a veil.

Civilization both veils and reveals. It reveals through great works that unmask, explore depths, and bring the unseen to daylight. The machine has the opposite effect: it veils nothing that is visible, and reveals nothing that is unseen. With some exceptions, electronic images remain on the surface of things; they show only the most external world, that in which all manifestations are alike, where the public peace of a free country is no different from the public peace of an enslaved one, where wounds to the soul are left in darkness, where center stage is left largely to the social comedy. Molière unmasked imposters, but Tartuffe has nothing to fear from our cameras. The images transmitted by the machine are not only easy to manipulate; they are also a marvelous tool for allowing oneself to be taken in by appearances. The image offered by technology is not the image forged by the artist; in general it cannot speak justly, unless a just text provides its meaning. Technology obscures our vision when it goes beyond its status as servant.

4. *Information is pure.* Information merely reflects what is going on in the world. And yet the facts that are reported have been sorted, singled out, ranked among a myriad of other facts—but by what criterion? Enough events happen in the world that a single day could supply enough information to last until the end of time. So why choose to report that an index has gone up, a record has fallen, or a plane has crashed, rather than to report that there are children crying, loves being born, and stars dying? The hierarchy of information reflects an interpretation of reality, but the myth of pure information relieves us of the obligation to justify this interpretation.

In practice, makeshift solutions seem to prevail, but only within limits set by unwritten laws. These laws, all of which bear the imprint of equality by default, are essentially the following: on the one hand, the rules (already noted) that follow the instrumental logic of the machine—ever more information, more speed, more images, more spectacle; on the other, a law that directly reflects the spirit of the times—the preference for "the epic of man as a physical being" (Bonald). The machine favors the economy, sports, health, sexuality—in a word, our bodily humanity, detached from any consideration of our true purpose. The spirit of late modernity rules the airwaves, and the elite group made up of television journalists draws from this spirit a feeling of irresponsibility that enhances their feeling of power.[2]

What does all this amount to, this flood of images and of news, this vast expenditure of means, effort, and energy? Very little, it appears, in terms of knowledge. This enormous machine has a trivial output. How many of us remember what was important (that is, what was considered important) a generation, a year, or a month ago? Everything passes, everything fades away, nothing really remains but crumbs, scraps of knowledge.[3] How could it be otherwise, when the machine dislocates time and space and endlessly vomits a stream of images and news? To borrow Shakespeare's golden words, the course of the world as seen through the machine comes down to this: "a tale, told by an idiot, full of sound and fury, signifying nothing." It follows that the machine accomplishes one feat of prowess after another in order to gain a few seconds in reporting what will be forgotten tomorrow. At the pace that has now become the rule, journalists are like so many hurried or crazed Sisyphuses; each moment's work must be done again the next moment, and none of this benefits anyone. The machine has gone mad.

2

The machine brings little benefit; indeed, it distorts much. It participates in the instrumental rationalization of the world and thus contributes what it can—that is, very much indeed—to changing the face of the world. It produces a dislocated image of the world, and then converts it into a spectacle for home delivery, a spectacle that tends to cut man off from his own world. The world-spectator has the illusion of looking at the world from above, but his vision is clouded.

The machine objectifies the world that it presents; it transforms it into an object at the disposal of man-as-spectator. As a result, as soon as I sit in front of my screen, I adopt a relation to the world unlike that of ordinary life. This world, the images of which are paraded before me, is a world I take seriously; I have the feeling that it is really today's world. But I also take it to be a world exterior to myself, a world that I see from the outside. I take it this way, first of all, because this is not the world in which I live from day to day, which is a world that does not extend to the Indian Ocean or to the president. If someone I know personally or a story on my neighborhood should appear on the screen, then immediately something clicks and my way of looking changes. And this is also because my position in a way puts me on the sidelines. I am separated from what is being shown to me; I see without being seen, I have no stake in the matter, I am a spectator. As Gabriel Marcel wrote, the objectification of the world severs the umbilical cord that ties man to what surrounds him. The machine does not so much connect me with the world as it invites me to feel independent from the world.

That is not all. Thanks to the machine, I seem, in a way, to be above the world. As a spectator, I take on the attitude of an outside observer and have (or seem to have) a sovereign freedom. I am at home, in my slippers, taking a bite out of an apple, and a simple push of a button allows me to interrupt one show and choose another; I am the master. The machine liberates the spectator from any respect for forms and subjects the whole range of human activity and work to the same attitude. "No work is so admirable, no catastrophe so terrible, no word so instructive as to cause one to stop eating an apple and addressing the screen in a familiar voice."[4] Thus everything touched by the machine is laid on a Procustean bed: not only is everything inserted into a ceaseless flux, but everything can be watched in slippers. Nothing is worth the trouble of stopping, nothing deserves to escape from the camera, that is, from the man in slippers on the other side. The machine homogenizes and debases the world. Everything is visible and subject to being on view: the president or Madonna, a criminal trial or a baseball game. The machine is a powerful auxiliary to equality by default; it levels the world. In so doing, it lifts me up as a spectator in relation to this world put at my disposal. Seated in front of my screen, I participate in the technological mastery of the world. I am above it and attend to it as I wish. My ego finds this quite satisfying.

Unfortunately, man-as-spectator is living an illusion. He believes that the machine is at his service; he feels more or less consciously that with the help of the machine he is able to raise himself up to a viewpoint superior to the world, when in fact he is falling into a trap: the machine produces alienation. Thanks to the information machine, the external world no longer stops at the threshold of the home; it penetrates, it resounds, it invades intimacy, and it does so in the form of a scintillating and meaningless spectacle. Man-as-spectator, who consumes every God-given day his portion of tele-vised news, distances himself from his own world in order to open the door to a foreign world devoid of meaning. As Jacques Ellul has written,

> For the recipient, this endless and massive news is often
> of no real, vital interest (in the strong sense of the term,
> of course, since it can be very "interesting" or even
> exciting!). He hears and sees innumerable things that do
> not at all concern him, things that can neither alert him
> nor serve any utilitarian, ideological, or spiritual pur-
> pose he might have. . . . He is invaded by absence.[5]

This "absence" invades the field of consciousness. The incessant
flux of news and the glistening of images tire, desiccate, and
encumber the mind. The whole enterprise of the machine is
founded on this false idea: that it is possible and beneficial to follow,
to absorb, to understand everything that is happening in the world
day by day. But no: this is impossible even if one devoted all one's
time to it, and there are many more important things to do. "One
must choose one's areas of ignorance," Gide liked to say. But the
machine is ignorant of what should be ignored, and the man-as-
spectator who is taken in by it turns his attention away from what
matters and wastes his time and strength. The external world presses
in, enervates, dissipates his psychic energy; it tends to absorb what
might have been available for reflection, for attention to others, for
the inner life. By watching without participating, without assimi-
lating, without ordering, by giving himself over to a flux of fleeting
sensations, man-as-spectator becomes blind to living realities. His
vision becomes tired, his sensitivity is muted, he loses the ability to
look at beings and things appropriately—with openness, simplicity,
and respect. He loses the ability to marvel, to be surprised, to be
moved by the world, to commune with those close to him or to be
touched by a great work of art, the ability to enter into himself by
silencing the racket of the outside world. The machine boasts of
allowing an "opening onto the world," but its tendency is quite to
the contrary: the closing of the world. Technology overlooks the fact
that what matters most for knowledge or understanding is not the
technical tool, however well developed it may be, but one's attitude
toward the world.

This opening-closing to the world is never so evident as when the spectator becomes the voyeur. Equality by default and the logic of the machine (justified by the "right to information") open all doors. The idea of transgression belongs to another day; everything now is open to view, even what used to be protected by the sanctuary of intimacy: sex, suffering, and death. And yet certain images wound us.

It is 1985. In Colombia, following a volcanic eruption, little Omayra is stuck in the mud and slowly sinking. The cameras are there, broadcasting live, all over the world, the agony of the little girl's death. Instrumental reason is proud of itself: what a great technical achievement! Each function is suitably fulfilled: while the child suffers in agony, the cameraman attends to the lighting and looks for the best angle, the control room selects the best pictures, and the commentator keeps on commenting. The human functions are up to the job; they offer the whole world a choice spectacle.

The little girl perishes beneath the gaze of millions of spectators. Does all this attention help her to die? If she were fully aware of what was happening, she would have to feel dispossessed, stripped of part of her being, transformed into an object. Her death no longer belongs to her and to those close to her; it has become a possession of millions of anonymous beings. When someone is dying, the only appropriate presence is the presence of those who are concerned by this death, who suffer with or help the one who is dying. The external observer has no place on such an occasion.

But here the external observers are numerous, and, thanks to the wonders of technology, they are invisible and comfortably settled in, looking through a two-way mirror with their behinds on couches and their feet in slippers. Why are they watching? To look at such images, it is impossible not to feel out of place; and yet I continue to watch, I succumb to a temptation, the one of which Socrates spoke that drove Leontis to take in the view of corpses despite his shame.[6] I succumb because television allows me to be indiscreet at little cost, allows me to satisfy an acknowledged curiosity. The machine transforms suffering and death into a spectacle, and I let myself be taken in by this spectacle because it brings me the satisfactions of voyeurism. In so doing I strip someone else of her dignity; I fail to respect her and to respect myself. In taking part in this business that objectifies what should not be objectified, I close myself to vital meanings; I adopt a brutal viewpoint on the world. At the first production of Racine's *Britannicus*, the audience was thin because at the same moment the Marquis of Courboyer was being executed in the Place de Grève. The process of civilization later led to the banning of public executions. But the machine "decivilizes."

The little girl dies, swallowed up by the mud. The broadcast ends. The normal schedule of programming resumes. And now, a commercial message.

PART THREE

THE FOOL'S BARGAIN

CHAPTER 13
THE MESS OF POTTAGE

1

The catechism of late modernity recapitulates the official rules that are in place in the world of equality by default. Its essence can be expressed in these ten commandments:

1. Thy Self alone shalt thou worship and love wholly.
2. All masters shalt thou reject and refuse absolutely.
3. Thy preferences shalt thou take as a rule of life uniquely.
4. The other shalt thou take as thy likeness exactly.
5. Thy rights shalt thou cultivate in every domain jealously.
6. Science shalt thou consider to be reason exclusively.
7. Procedures shalt thou respect, but forms neglect freely.
8. Technology shalt thou employ to serve thee abundantly.
9. The world shalt thou regard as thy possession entirely.
10. Modern shalt thou be in every respect superbly.

2

These commandments, which apply equally to everyone, amount above all to one thing: "You are a master. Act accordingly." Or, more precisely, "You are a master. You must behave as such in two ways: you must be your own creator, and be assured that, whatever your choices may be, no one is greater than yourself. And you must get an upper hand on the world, apply technoscientistic reason, become a specialist, dominate your object. Let nothing hold you back. Nothing is given but your radical autonomy; you owe nothing to anyone." Modern man is intoxicated, carried away by these words.

3

The transition takes place as follows: late modernity leads to two attitudes, one subjectivist, the other dominating, and both contribute to a feeling of power. Moral subjectivism wipes the slate clean, overturning all objective rules, universal imperatives, examples, and models—each person must invent his own "values," discover his own "authenticity" through self-expression. As Charles Taylor observes, "The understanding of value as created gives a sense of freedom and power."[1] In other words: henceforth I am my only master; there is no one to admire, no one to listen to, no one to imitate; I have no norms but those I give myself. I am free not only to live as I wish but also to determine absolutely the value of my actions. I do what I want to do and I am worth what I say I am worth. Regardless of the object of my will, my pure will itself suffices. Thus modern man is filled with a feeling of exaltation, but this exaltation is empty of any content. The Self has taken its place.

The Self also swells up in taking on the attitudes encouraged by technoscience. When modern man plays the pure expert in his profession, when he uses in conversation the vague and scholarly vocabulary of the social sciences, when he takes up the command of modern machines, he seems to grow, he takes himself for a superior being. As an expert or apprentice expert he assumes a certain distance from the world, and as the user of technology he is the master of formidable means in which the might of modern knowledge is embodied. Armed with science or with technique, he is not a person devoted to some service, but someone endowed with power. The pure expert defines himself not only as someone who possesses technoscientific competence, but also as someone who needs no external authority: technical competence is self-sufficient; it follows its own logic, it is autonomous. It matters little for the satisfaction of the ego that this power has no true compass. What matters is less the object of the will than the will itself.

Let us take an example from the human world, where getting the upper hand means getting the upper hand on human beings. Take the case of a doctor of the old school. He depends, to be sure, on his scientific training, but he also depends on his human experience. Through this experience, he is on the same footing with his patient, he is a person caring for another person. Now consider a young doctor keen on techniques and nothing else. He sees in the patient only the bearer of a defective organ; he shares nothing with him, he views him from a distance, with cold competence. The expert boasts a kind of knowledge in which the Self has no part, but on the basis of this same knowledge, he considers himself apart from and above ordinary people. Impersonal knowledge disengages the human being but satisfies the Self. In other words, *the self is in the very method*; it is in a certain attitude in relation to the world and to others.

The same analysis holds true for the sociologist, the nurse, the economist, the teacher. To the degree that they abstract from or disregard their human condition in order to take on a technical form of knowledge, they disengage themselves and ascend to the heights. The sociologist wraps himself in his jargon in order to crush vital distinctions in utterly complacent irresponsibility; the nurse looks at things clinically and sets aside her gown as soon as her shift ends; the teacher is intoxicated with the sophisticated jargon of modern pedagogy and tends to consider the teaching of spelling as beneath him.[2] As the icy knowledge of the expert invades human relations, the Self tends to deal with its fellow human beings from a position of superiority. The rational mastery of the world offers many satisfactions to the person who approaches humanity technologically, even if he himself may suffer from these same techniques when he in turn becomes their object.

4

Possessing both irrational freedom and rational mastery, modern man feels the power of his will. He is a master. To adapt a famous saying, the catechism of late modernity is Nietzscheanism for the people. But is it not also a fool's bargain? When contemporary man accedes to the sirens of the spirit of the age, he encloses himself in his illusions; he gives himself over to a pretense. The commandments of late modernity are not such as to make free minds. Modern man sells his soul for a mess of pottage.

CHAPTER 14
DISARMED MASTERS

The destiny of humanity by default can be briefly stated: by making himself a master, man loses the means to order his life; more profoundly, he loses the possibility to become what he is. He believes he is bettering himself; he disarms himself. The commandments of late modernity are filled with illusions, and these illusions operate as a snare. When modern man sets out to be self-sufficient in keeping with equality by default's injunction of autonomy, he denies his condition as a human being and finds himself naked before a world stripped of meaning. When he adopts the cold and dominating attitude encouraged by scientific reason and modern technique, he equips himself only with fragments of knowledge that have nothing to say about the art of living and cut him off from all vital knowledge. As he makes sacrifices to the Self, he thus closes himself off and strips himself of his own knowledge as a person of flesh and blood, as a human being endowed with a conscience and facing up to the realities of existence. The apprentice master does not know his own ignorance and he is ignorant of what he knows. He is without resources. So what does he do? He lives at a distance from himself, he plays a role, he poses.

1

"I owe nothing to no one," says default man, and he did not come up with this idea by himself. "I am born free, I am independent and sovereign by natural right." It would be hard to go further astray, to push the sin of ingratitude any further. The truth is the opposite: man is a being to whom much has been given—his life, his humanity, his inherited aptitudes, his language, his education, the world that receives him and everything that is available thanks to the work of those who have preceded him. Man does not owe his existence to himself. He belongs to a biological order and a human lineage without which he would not exist.[1] Nor would he exist if those who gave him life (or, as the case may be, someone else) had not cared for him at the time of his birth and during his period of extreme dependency. Moreover, man does not make himself; he cannot become what he is without the care and the educational contributions of others. The child left alone who miraculously survives becomes a "wild child"; in the absence of socialization, his humanity remains a fallow field. In other words, to recall a truth as old as Aristotle, man is by nature a social being; among all the things he needs, the first is other people.

Man is also an heir in another sense. The world was not born with him; when he enters it his heritage includes what past generations have discovered and accumulated. Contemporary man receives so much that it would take volumes to make an inventory. Here are just a few examples: modern man knows that the earth is round—he hasn't verified this himself. He uses an alphabet that he did not create. He uses electricity, which he did not invent. He is cured with antibiotics, which he did not discover. He rides a bicycle, which he did not design. He enjoys political liberty, which he did not found. The fundamental fact of transmission makes each of us the beneficiary of innumerable gifts. As Bertrand de Jouvenel said, every self-aware person sees himself as a debtor.

2

The apprentice master is not, as he claims to be, autonomous, and by pursuing autonomy he dispossesses himself. The will to radical autonomy imposes certain constraints. One who sees himself as supremely free is not free to choose a master or a model; he is the measure of his own good, and he intends to find it by himself. "The great problem for human beings," Jacques Maritain wrote, "is to find a master." How can default man, who wants to be his own master, accept another? He objects indignantly—this idea is an offense against equality—or with indifference—this idea is too ridiculous to take seriously. Each person knows no rule but his own autonomous and sovereign opinion; therefore, as we have seen, all authority is authoritatively challenged, even the authority of great minds whose dialogue informs our culture and our institutions (religion, higher education, and the like). More or less consciously, default man in his vanity refuses all support and all guidance; he turns inward and "claims to judge the world" (Tocqueville).

This closing goes even further. The will to autonomy raises a barrier that shuts out not only all authority but more generally all vital knowledge. In the realm of opinion, there is no place for an understanding that engages being. What is opinion? It belongs to the order of having; it is something that I possess, something that depends only on my sovereign freedom, something that is not essential to what I am. "You will notice," Gabriel Marcel wrote, "that, where beings of which we have an intimate understanding are concerned, we do not, properly speaking, have opinions. We can see this with reference to the works of artists, etc. If someone asked my opinion of Mozart or of Wagner, I would not know how to answer; it is as if my experience has too much depth, as if my spiritual cohabitation with Mozart or Wagner were too close."[2] There are countless examples of this: Andromache has no opinion on Hector or on Astyanax, any more than Titus has an opinion on Rome or Polyeucte on God. They do not express an opinion; instead they bear witness. If I were to say, "Here is my opinion on my son," then

I am distancing myself, I am severing an essential bond, I am excluding my son from the circle of my being. More generally, all profound experience is foreign to the language of opinion: would a survivor of a Nazi camp say, "Here is my opinion on what I lived through"? But testimony engages us. What I gain in being I lose in having. When being is involved, what is does not depend on my sovereign freedom; rather, I participate in, I attest to, something that is not dependent on me, something of which I am not the master. The reign of the Self requires us to remain on the surface and on the outside. *Opinion is at once self-affirmation and disengagement from being.* Default man knows nothing from the inside.

3

Scientistic reason tends in the same direction; it takes away much more than it gives. Pure, hard science, as we have already emphasized, joins forces with the radical will to autonomy in denying all vital understanding. Because it claims to embody reason as a whole, it keeps it within its own walls and thus consecrates the sovereignty of opinion in all areas outside its domain, those that have to do with the art of living. The man who knows is the one who wears the robes of method; humanity knew nothing before this absolute beginning. The scientistic sciences—in particular the human sciences—not only disqualify the knowledge embodied in culture and institutions. They also strip ordinary people of all knowledge.

It follows that the more people play the role of experts, and the more people listen to experts, the more they dispossess themselves, the more they abdicate their status as human beings. "Let all join us in the camp of true knowledge," says scientistic or technoscientistic reason. "But, in order to do this, leave behind the old man and get rid of all you thought you knew by your own means. We don't want to hear talk of common sense or practical wisdom. Ordinary people are endowed with no natural insight—there are no primary truths, no natural evidence in the intellectual or sensible or moral realms. As for practice, it has nothing to teach without the assistance of science. What some call the experience of life's profound realities has no value. Man has nothing to learn from his ordinary misfortunes (growing old, losing his parents, approaching death); fathers and mothers learn nothing in raising their children, and peasants have never learned anything from their battle with nature. In a word, living teaches nothing at all. In order to know something, please consult the technical manuals."

Experts and apprentice experts are truncated human beings who remind us of Montesquieu's saying: "I love peasants; they're not learned enough to reason crosswise." In the world of equality by default, this kind of education or rather this half-education which has the effect of "devitalizing," of desiccating the mind, becomes the rule. People distance themselves from their natural understanding and from everything taught by organic experience; they turn away from culture and are left in between, with no knowledge except what has been dissociated from life. Yet on the other hand, this knowledge is power, and its method is such as to satisfy the ego. In the kingdom of pure science, as in the kingdom of opinion, the Self wins and being loses. *Scientistic reason is at once self-affirmation and disengagement from being.* Default man knows nothing but from the outside.

4

Default man is not only disarmed by this will to autonomy and this grip of the scientistic or technoscientistic attitude; he is also turned away from thinking. When subjectivism reigns, there are no longer good reasons to reflect on one's life. Why exercise one's reason when a choice founded on reason is worth no more than the most futile choice, when a reasonable feeling has the same value as an unreasonable one, when the rules of life are purely arbitrary? Choices lose all significance, they affect nothing that matters, they are not serious. "To be or not to be?" Hamlet's question is of the same order as "White or red wine?" and it calls for the same response: no matter, to each his own. Choice is, in every sense of the word, meaningless. If every choice contains its own justification, if it has no foundation but pure subjectivity, then the absurd reigns.

It is important to distinguish between the freedom to choose and the freedom to determine the value of one's choices. Pure freedom implies both: I am free to choose between nobility and baseness or between courage and cowardice and I am also free to believe that baseness is as good as nobility or cowardice as good as courage. I am free to decide that what gives my life meaning is bungee jumping or building biceps of steel. What is significant depends on my will. As concerns me, I am master of the questions that matter, of the things that are worthwhile. Under these conditions, as Charles Taylor forcefully observed, nothing is in itself meaningful and freedom is deprived of all meaning.[3] In order for my freedom to take on meaning, my freedom must be situated within an ordered and hierarchical framework; the choices I make must have some relation to rules that are independent of my will: I can choose between cowardice and courage but the value of my choice is not up to me. In other words, *free choice has meaning only if I am not the master of meaning*. The spirit of the age does not share this view. Opinion is king; it determines the value of things; each man is himself the master of meaning, the master of a meaning without significance.

5

The commandments of late modernity thus function as a fool's bargain: they offer a feeling of power at the price of abdication. The apprentice master condemns himself to live and die incapable of distinguishing what matters from what does not, what is meaningful from what is not. He condemns himself to live without reflecting on his life. Default man believes himself to be a master, and he is disarmed. So what does he do? He plays at being the apprentice master, he "plays smart," as Péguy would say; without being aware of it, he reads from a script. What motivates him is not a thought endowed with content, nor a will striving toward an end; it is the will to decide for himself, simply in order to decide for himself, the pure will to give effect to his will. Default man desires nothing so ardently as this: he wills to will, to exercise his sovereign subjectivity. He wants to be autonomous for the sake of autonomy. He is a man without a cause who is intoxicated or satisfied with this arbitrary power that he believes he confers upon his will. No matter the object or the content. What matters is the procedure. What the genius of Tocqueville discerned so long ago has never been truer than under late modernity: the man taken in by the spirit of the age is not very attached to his opinion, but he is determined to have an opinion; he is not very attached to what he says, but he insists on having "something to say."

On the other hand, when default man adopts the attitude of the expert, what is he doing but playing a role? He silences a part of himself, he adopts a pose that allows him to dominate his object. The pure expert is pure will; he is indifferent to the goals he pursues and does not question those goals. All who follow or imitate him embrace the same viewpoint. Here as before, human beings who heed the sirens of the spirit of the age distance themselves from themselves.

6

Default man plays a role, and this role is dictated from the outside. The apprentice master challenges all authority; he avoids committing himself wholly, so he is defenseless against influences. Now what influence is more powerful than that which bears the seal of common opinion and thus in no way offends equality? The spirit of the age tells him repeatedly: "Be a master, be like everyone else. Be a master, be of your times"—and so he opines without seeing the contradiction. Late-modern man closes himself up in late modernity. How can he escape it, since he knows only one way of seeing and thinking, a way that deprives him of all vital understanding? How can he escape it, now that he has cut the Ariadne's thread of culture and so knows nothing of the great choices of human life? He lacks the means to distance himself from the ruling or dominant opinion. He believes himself to be autonomous, and he is conformist. By trying to be a master, he puts himself under the influence of the spirit of the age and of what that spirit takes for granted. Among the virtues most alien to modern man is the virtue of wonder: the modern world and the modern vision of the world are accepted as if they were natural. But whoever cannot experience wonder surrenders himself bound hand and foot.

CHAPTER 15

ROLE PLAYING

1

The student is looking at a blank piece of paper. He has been asked to write about one of those subjects which today's schools are so fond of, a question that has to do with a "social problem" or some current issue: "the role of the media," "ways to fight religious and racial intolerance," "issues in communication," "the reign of fashion," "the new South Africa," etc. Test questions like these are not at all surprising, yet they differ profoundly from traditional school exercises (especially in France). Their object is different: here the school rejects any stepping back and any indirection. Rather, the student is immersed in what is current and immediate. And the school's method is even more different: it has abdicated its traditional mission of forming the capacity for judgment. The question posed is new for the student as a student; it is the subject of an examination without being the subject of teaching. The adolescent must decide for himself and give an opinion, which it is assumed he must have—he is somehow officially held to possess the means to pass judgment. The teacher limits himself to testing that capacity to express a judgment, which itself has no need of enlightenment. Thus the school surrenders twice to the information machine. First, it involves itself in questions of current events and reinforces the disproportionate importance the machine accords them rather than assuming the distance proper to its role. Next, it abandons its own rules of method—treating questions systemically, methodically, and progressively—in favor of those which govern the machine and are in harmony with the rule of opinion—treating questions in no particular order, on the assumption that they are immediately intelligible to everyone. So get to work, student, and come up with your own opinion.

But the student has no means to do this. The problems at issue are far from immediately intelligible, so far indeed that an adult who had followed a thousand news stories and debates on the subject would have great difficulty defining the key terms: What exactly, for example, is meant by *racism*? What exactly is the scope of the term *communication*? How could one imagine for a single moment that an adolescent could find his way all alone where even prominent public discussions often get bogged down in uncertainties of vocabulary? The student is disarmed. What does he do? Unable to think for himself, he endeavors to think as one is supposed to think. He looks to whatever is within easy reach, especially the mood of the day; he presents received opinions as if they were his own. He puts on the attitude required by the exercise, and plays the role required by his fictitious autonomy. What he writes matters little to him really, but he is learning some bad habits: to judge without knowing, to decide without bothering to clarify, to trust in accepted opinion, and to present it as his own. He is unlearning a fundamental rule of independence of mind: the suspension of judgment when thought does not have the resources to make a pronouncement. The exercise is supposed to develop a critical spirit—the official instructions make this very clear—but its tendency is the contrary, since it fails to respect the principle applied by Pascal's father in educating his son, a principle valid for everything involved in learning how to think: one should offer to the child's understanding what he is capable of understanding.

Education has often ignored this rule, and students did not of course wait for late modernity in order to play their required roles, some more than others. But here is what is new: it is in the name of an exercise in autonomy that the school here asks too much and in the wrong way, and thus invites pretense. In other words, it is the conversion of the right to an opinion into the duty to an opinion that grounds the institutionalization of fakery. While classes in literature or languages imitate the opinion-mongering of talk shows, while everyone plays the role of autonomous subject, the schools fabricate appearances; they strive to fabricate or reinforce an illusion. They are part and parcel of the social comedy that is played out on the stage of equality by default.

2

The survey researcher and subject are face to face. The researcher is affable; he explains calmly the purpose of the survey. The subject concentrates and takes his position. He is not at all surprised—there are so many surveys, on every conceivable subject. Being questioned in this way and on this theme among a thousand other possibilities seems as natural as can be. The subject accepts the proposed rules of the game without batting an eye—all the more so because he is flattered by the status conferred upon him. He experiences some satisfaction in seeing his opinion recognized, held to be equal to any other, on its way to becoming, as it were, official in the form of a statistical datum. But now the preparations are over, and it is time to get serious. His brow furrows. The questions posed to him have no relation to what he thinks about; they are a thousand miles from his concerns and his experience. He is asked, for example, "Do you believe that the United Nations has worked effectively to improve world health?" (Roper, 1981); "Do you believe that in coming years the number of forest fires will increase or decrease?" (SOFRES, France, 1987); "Do you believe that Gorbachev is sincere in calling for a reduction of nuclear arms?" (Gallup, 1987); "Do you favor or oppose the establishment of a single European currency?" (B.V.A.

France, 1993); "Do you think Bill Clinton's actions as U.S. president will have a positive effect, a negative effect, or no effect on the world economy?" (SOFRES, France, 1993). The subject is perplexed. What can he do? The only reasonable response would be to acknowledge ignorance. But to choose not to respond would be a kind of abdication, a renunciation of his opinion; it would be like lowering the flag of autonomy. Furthermore, why deprive himself? Opinions cost nothing, they imply no commitment, they involve no obligation whatsoever. So the subject does what the survey machine asks. He gives the answers he thinks are considered appropriate (unlike voting, survey research is not secret); he chooses one of the answers that have been so conveniently prepared for his use. The researcher, whose attitude attests to the importance he attaches to the opinion of his interlocutor, sighs a deep, comforting sigh and scrupulously checks off the right box. If by some misfortune the scale seems to tip toward the wrong choice (no response), he applies more pressure, he tries again, he insists as skillfully as he can in order to obtain what his function demands—his task is to reduce as far as possible the number of nonresponses. The great enemy of survey research is the suspension of judgment. What would become of polls if everyone limited themselves to what they knew? Fortunately those surveyed play along, and those who refuse are never more than a small minority, even in cases where reason would dictate massive abstention. Recall the examples dealing with UN policy, forest fires, Gorbachev's sincerity, etc. The percentage of nonresponses ranged from 9 to 21 percent—in other words, the response rate was never below 79 percent. What a great success! Little matter that the recorded opinion is inconsistent and that sometimes this inconsistency comes to light in the form of an evident incoherence.[1]

The surveyor and the surveyed part company in contentment. They have worked together well; they have created out of whole cloth an opinion that did not exist a few minutes before, an opinion that, combined with all the other opinions of the same caliber, will be consecrated "public opinion." The subject has the satisfaction of a job well done; he has fulfilled his duty to have an opinion, his duty of autonomy. But without realizing or fully realizing it, he has shackled his independence of mind in the name of this very independence. Who is the free man—the one who says "I do not know" when he does not know, or the one who pretends to know? Socrates' lesson is always relevant.

Does any of this shake the confidence of the researcher? Hardly, it appears. He holds a trump card and does not hesitate to play it: "You're forgetting one thing that refutes what you say. What do you make of preelection polls? Here the evidence is irrefutable. Will you deny the overwhelming confirmation provided by election results (leaving aside a few blunders)? We have given proof of our expertise and of the validity of our techniques. All the rest is just talk." To be sure, the preceding examples do not tell the whole story; this can be conceded. But does the validity of surveys having to do with voters' intentions and conducted on the eve of an election guarantee the validity of all others? Not at all. Distinctions must be made. All the opinions gathered by survey research are not equally consistent, just as they are not equally sincere.[2] One must distinguish among subjects (and among surveys, according to how carefully they are designed), and surveys that are the hallmark of specialized institutes are a special case. The first reason is this: the response confirmed by election results is given just a few days before the election, that is, at the end of an election campaign and as the decisive day is approaching. This response expresses an intention to vote a certain way; it takes a form that surprises no one, and the question is modeled on what the citizen must soon do and which he is in the habit of doing. In other words, these opinions are expressed in a simple and familiar framework and in a context characterized by intense public debate on the question at hand and by the proximity of an impending choice that will decide the question and determine the future of all concerned. How could such opinions not be more consistent than those which make up the stock in trade of most other surveys? And there are three other reasons that contribute to the accuracy of responses: (1) The transition from expressing an opinion to actually voting costs nothing. In other areas this is not always so: a generous opinion costs nothing, but not so a generous attitude; (2) There is a margin of dissimulation, but this is checked and corrected by various ad hoc procedures. The repetition of surveys and the simplicity and familiarity of the questions facilitate reliability; (3) More generally, these surveys are conducted with very special caution. The research organizations have a lot at stake, even their very credibility. They know this, and so they take extra care. The validity of surveys conducted close, very close, to elections cannot be generalized to other surveys. Not all surveys are of the same quality.

The result is that there are surveys that deceive hardly at all, there are those that deceive on a large scale, and then there are all the intermediate cases in which surveys are more or less deceptive without it being possible to know just how deceptive they are. If the survey machine functions in all cases, this is because the people questioned speak when they know what they think, and also because they believe they are bound to speak when they do not know what they think. In order to declare opinion king as expressed through expert techniques, techniques must be blind or choose to blind themselves, and opinion must be in bondage.

3

In broadcasting, the social comedy may be said to have its own rites. We have already discussed them, but let us recall certain key points. Every evening, the curtain rises on what is, at least in part, a bit of theater: the star anchor who presents the television news takes on the attitude of one who knows all there is to know about world affairs. With a calm yet firm voice and a clear-eyed look, he never hesitates, doubt never seems to enter his mind; he embodies a tranquil certainty. Who has ever heard him admit ignorance, voice perplexity, recommend the suspension of judgment? He does what the machine wants him to do, he carries on "as if." And he invites his invisible interlocutor to do the same: the machine makes the course of world events visible and comprehensible—who would dare confess himself incapable of grasping its meaning? Man-as-spectator has his own role to play in this comedy. Apparently, he plays that role seriously.

4

Schools (or certain school exercises), surveys (or many of them), broadcast news (or much of it)—in all three cases the individual is invited to adopt a self-serving and artificial pose. He is put or he puts himself in the position of having to judge the world all by himself and in terms that are foreign. These are terms that he has not chosen, that generally appeal to some impersonal, external body of knowledge, and that cast personal knowledge, knowledge of man as man, knowledge forged by vital experience, into darkness. In other words, the rules of the game are not innocent. Each and every person must express himself, but according to the proper attitude. A person should speak out, but only in the name of pure freedom or to repeat the view of an expert. Let him detach himself from his essential humanity and from his organic experience. In a word, he must be stripped of his being for the benefit of his Self. The rule of opinion and of scientistic reason is not the emancipation of the common man but his abdication in favor of a new man shaped from the outside. Those Péguy called "little people" are not asked to change their way of being in order to enter into the world of culture; instead they are required to cease being themselves in order to fit into the world of radical autonomy and cold expertise. The cult of opinion is compatible with contempt for "little people."

Thus the dice are loaded. The apprentice master, a victim of the scripted role he plays, cultivates a triple ignorance, the very same that Socrates brought to light so well: he does not know what he is talking about, he does not know that he does not know, and he no longer even knows what he knows. He is primed to follow the path prepared for him. It is no accident that so-called autonomous men are so much alike.

CHAPTER 16
THE UNEQUAL EQUALITY OF OPINIONS

The catechism of late modernity is, in a way, an official text. But it does not say everything; there is more. The spirit of the age preaches a relativist dogmatism and a scientistic dogmatism that cannot be taken to their logical conclusions: pure freedom and immaculate reason are not only myths, they also destroy themselves. This internal contradiction points toward a hidden side of the spirit of the age: late modernity does not follow through on its own principles; it speaks out of both sides of its mouth. On the one hand, relativism comes into play when opposing "values" are at stake; on the other hand, it gives way where fashionable and conformist opinions are concerned. In the first case the dominant discourse says, "Everyone lives as he thinks best"; in the second, "Here is the preferred way to live." There is no *bona vita* according to reason, but there is a how-you're-supposed-to-live according to the spirit of the age. As in Orwell's *Animal Farm*, all opinions are equal, but some are more equal than others.

This dominant discourse presents itself as the expression of commonly held opinion, which Tocqueville says takes the place of dogma in modern societies. But here again there is some pretense (which Tocqueville's penchant for general ideas and "democratic" interpretations led him to overlook). While it is true that opinion rules, this ruling or dominant opinion, this socially appropriate opinion, this opinion which can be expressed in public without need of justification and without risk of opprobrium—this public opinion, finally, if one accepts Elisabeth Noelle-Neumann's definition,[1] does not first appear as commonly held opinion. It claims to embody that opinion, but in fact it tends to shape it from the outside. In the genesis and the orchestration of dominant opinion, some people have more weight than others. All opinions are equal, but some are more equal than others.

1

Late modernity proclaims the dogmas of equality without substance, formal rights, and pure freedom in the name of the relativity of choices, opinions, and ends. Such a relativistic dogmatism not only does violence to the human condition; it destroys itself. The logic of relativism is pitiless; it eventually undermines the dogmas it was meant to justify. Some kind of anchor is necessary, or else principles are founded on sand. Late modernity is poised on a slope that leads to its own destruction, along the paths of logic as well as psychology. There is no deviating from these paths once the fundamental principle underlying pure or indeterminate freedom is set in motion: "All choices are of equal worth."

If all choices are equal, I cannot rationally justify the choice of freedom, of equality, of democracy. If "values" are equal, how can I attribute a special status to the "value" of freedom or that of equality; in the name of what can I favor democracy over another regime? If opinions are equal, then opinions hostile to freedom, equality, and democracy are as good as those which are favorable to them. Moreover, if opinions are equal, then the opinion according to which opinions are unequal is as good as the opinion according to which they are equal. And so we find ourselves at an impasse.

If all choices are of equal worth, I can make the choice to alienate my freedom. Pure freedom is defenseless before itself: the free man is free to sell his body or his soul. John Stuart Mill rightly observed that man is not free to renounce his freedom because, if he were, he would be in a position to reduce to nothing the very justification of freedom itself. But Mill's proposition has meaning only if one admits that freedom is ordered according to man's humanity, that it is something besides an indeterminate freedom. Pure or formal freedom can be freely abolished, just as formal democracy can be democratically abolished. If democracy is reduced to the procedures by which the will of the majority is expressed, then a majority vote is sufficient to abrogate democracy. In Athens in 411 B.C., the popular assembly decided to bring an end to the democratic regime.

If all choices are equivalent, I must reject the rights of man understood as universal rights. Every "culture" is original and irreducible; none can be said to be superior to another. How can one preach this cultural relativism without abandoning the universalism of rights? Of all the contradictions with which relativistic dogmatism is riven, this is the most visible because it is inscribed in practice: when it comes to foreign "cultures," the modern mind is torn. On the one hand, the universalism of rights compels us to advocate and to act such that these rights are respected everywhere. On the other hand, cultural relativism requires inaction or passivity in the name of respect for the sovereign particularity of each "culture." Thought through to its conclusions, this relativism leads to the following: no one can offer care, education, or protection except at home, and the cannibal has a "right to be different."

If all choices are equivalent, I leave the field open to the enemies of freedom (or equality, or democracy). Their choices are as valid as those of the friends of freedom. And I am myself not at all bound to respect the freedom of others, nor do I have anything to say to those who do not respect it. "These are my values," says one who is brutal, violent, and sadistic. If all "values" are equal, how can we answer him? Pure freedom knows no limit; nothing remains that I must respect, either my freedom or that of others. Pure freedom subverts everything, including freedom itself.

If all choices are equivalent, they no longer have any intrinsic value; they are not respectable—so why respect them? The relativism of choices, values, and opinions has a leveling effect: if everything has value, nothing does. Such a position does not really lead to respect for individual conscience. Modern man, who sees himself as the creator of his own "values," experiences a feeling of power—"I am my own master"; he hardly experiences a feeling of respect for himself or others. "The more one lowers the source of opinions, the more one sees them as vain shadows, and the less reason one has to respect them."[2] Psychology tends in the same direction as logic: pure freedom tends to subvert freedom.

2

Pure reason, cold, disembodied, and dominating reason, with which scientism arms itself, follows the same path as pure freedom, that of self-destruction. The proponent of scientism limits himself to demonstrative (logical or logico-empirical) reason, and relegates everything else to unscientific darkness. If he abides by his principles to the end, he should conclude: (1) My work has no meaning; and (2) My findings have no meaning. Skepticism, Pascal says, is but an avatar of rationalism; it is reason in the process of destroying itself with its own weapons.

Scientistic reason is neutral with respect to different "values"; it is thus neutral between ignorance and knowledge, intellectual probity and trickery, freedom of thought and tyranny over the mind. It follows that it can no more justify itself than it can justify the conditions of its exercise. Why use reason rather than abandon oneself to unreason? Why devote oneself to science rather than plunder? Pure science, which claims to be autonomous, is powerless to respond. Imagine a student in an auditorium suddenly standing up and declaring: "Professor, it is my honor to inform you that I have well assimilated the principles you have taught us (that reason cannot determine any norms) and that in the name of these same principles, I reject your way of doing things. You judge papers according to what you call their qualities of clarity, rigor, precision, and who knows what else. By what right—in the name of values the validity of which cannot be proven? Your values are worth no more than mine, and mine authorize me to say the following: 'If you do not give me an excellent grade on the test, I will unfortunately have to box your ears and break your nose.' And please do not answer that it is wrong to act this way and that violence is reprehensible. In making such judgments, you would be overstepping your own competence and contradicting yourself." What can the scientistic professor do except become aware, a bit belatedly, that he has been a sorcerer's apprentice?

Scientistic science cannot even validate its own findings. Aristotle, Pascal, and Bergson, among others, have shown that all demonstrations rest upon indemonstrable propositions. Knowledge is never immaculate; it rests finally on certain primary truths, that is to say, rational givens. If Bachelard's famous statement ("There are no primary truths, there are only primary errors") were true, then all scientific knowledge would collapse like a house of cards. Science that claims to be autonomous haughtily disqualifies ordinary knowledge, but in practice it cannot do without it. If reason is entirely demonstrative, it demonstrates nothing.

Take a mathematical proof. The result is not right unless the proof is. Thus it is necessary to prove the truth of the proof. But this second proof must itself be proved, and so on. Proof abandoned to itself is always incomplete. Reasoning reason, Bergson writes, "is incapable of proving its own veracity to itself, for it could only do so by using itself, that is by reasoning, and the question concerns precisely the legitimacy of such reasoning: we are going in circles. . . ."[3] The proof cannot succeed unless the evidence of its validity is compelling. In the absence of recourse to intelligible first principles (such as the principle of identity, the principle of noncontradiction) that are self-evident and ground the legitimacy of reasoning, nothing—absolutely nothing—can be proven.

Take an experimental proof. Like the mathematical proof, it is based on intellectual self-evidence. It is also based on physical self-evidence: i.e., that our senses tell the truth when they tell us that matter, noise, light, and so on, exist. What would science be if our senses were nothing but "deceiving powers," if the eye gave us the illusion of a reality that did not exist, if touch grasped nothing but a mirage? No one can prove the existence of an external world. Only the evidence of the senses provides such proof. It suffices for all reasonable human beings.

Science that knows itself must recognize the following: it is built on "humble foundations," as Chesterton said in commenting on Thomas Aquinas. The knowledge of the learned is worth nothing if it turns its nose up at the knowledge of the ignorant. So what do practitioners of scientism do? In general they proceed "as if"—as if science were autonomous—all the while depending on self-evident truths just like everyone else. Consider a scientific meeting proceeding in the scientistic fashion. The discussions are learned, and yet they presuppose a thousand things that have not been passed through the filter of method: that all the participants are not dreaming, that they perceive in the same way what is said or shown, that they reason in the same way, that they are not crazy. Must every participant prove that he is of sound mind? For the participants are not necessarily sane, especially if we take Chesterton's definition: the madman is not one who has lost his (reasoning) reason, but the one who has lost everything except his reason.

Scientists committed to scientism do not generally carry their principles to their logical conclusions. If they did, they would end up in the same place as contemporary epistemology: science cannot establish any truth; at the limit, the notion of truth itself has no meaning. The scientistic philosophy of science takes many paths: when it remains consistent with itself, it leads to skepticism. Yet the epistemologist lives like everyone else—he does not doubt his existence, that boiling water burns you, that night follows day, that his arguments stand up, and, if he is sick, that the doctor is in touch with objective reality. Like all scientistic thinkers, he thinks with only a part of himself. He ends up with unreasonable conclusions because he imprisons reason in the circle of method. But these conclusions have the virtue of showing logic at work: extreme rationalism ends up in irrationalism. Reason so conceived cannot speak of the Good, nor can it speak of the True. Pure reason subverts reason.[4]

3

Late modernity proclaims principles that it cannot completely follow without destroying itself. Why this contradiction? Blindness is no doubt a part of the reason, as is duplicity. Logical incoherence has its own logic that relativizes relativistic dogmatism. In other words, this contradiction points beyond itself to something else: late modernity says more than it says it says.

What does it say? It speaks two languages and practices a double standard. It proclaims the dogmas of relativism in order to do battle against rules of life it opposes, while at the same time it relaxes its relativism in order to present the "values" that define the new orthodoxy as if they were etched in stone. It claims to be beyond good and evil, while at the same time it redefines good and evil. It claims to be in favor of the equality of opinions, while at the same time it says which opinions are appropriate. This discourse is therefore contradictory, but it is also coherent: it is contradictory because its argumentation continually offends logic, and it is coherent because its prohibitions, its imperatives, and its incentives are in essential agreement on the way in which rules governing morals and manners should be changed.

The operation has three phases (which are logically if not chronologically distinct): (1) dominant opinion appeals to relativism and to the equality of opinions in order to discredit the idea of the good; (2) it appeals to egalitarian-libertarian dogmas in order to redefine appropriate opinions and attitudes, as well as those that are to be considered inappropriate and execrable; and (3) it appeals to the prejudices of modern historicism and to the appearance of a "democratic" opinion in order to give this new orthodoxy the seal of incontestability.

1. *Appeal to relativism and the equality of opinions.* As we have seen, the equality of opinion plays a subversive role. It disqualifies the idea of the "good life" such as it has been understood by the philosophic and religious tradition of the West. The inherited norms and models of civilization are henceforth classified under the rubric of opinions with the same status as the multitude of individual opinions. Relativistic dogmatism and scientistic dogmatism join forces to affirm that there is no good in itself. As a result, it is good to renounce the good. The new virtues have names such as "authenticity," "tolerance," "self-expression," "openness"—in other words "values" that are presented as neutral or "value-free" (in spite of the contradiction present in the terms) and claim to be in the service of pure freedom for oneself and others. It is implicitly or unconsciously understood that relativism stops at the principle that grounds it: the equality of opinions is not a matter of opinion but of dogma.

The effect of this discourse is to close up thought and to circumscribe the range of legitimate questions. Socrates is left without an interlocutor. He noticed already in the *Theatetus* that the practice of dialectical discussion lost all significance when man is considered the measure of all things—what is the good of discussing, reasoning, seeking answers together if all answers are equally valid? Reflection on the art of living as inaugurated by Socrates has no object; it is hardly even considered appropriate. It presupposes that the Good is beyond opinion, and so it offends the sovereign freedom of each person. Let it be said once and for all: reason is asked to limit itself to the sphere of authorized questions, which excludes the crucial questions. The mind is asked not to think about questions that matter. Sovereign freedom excludes the freedom to question freedom. Prejudice reigns.

2. *Appeal to egalitarian-libertarian dogmas.* The dominant discourse evades the relativism it professes in order to present the opinions and attitudes that define appropriate ways of being as unproblematic. This new version of the *bona vita* essentially has two components: it combines *practical egoism* with *egalitarian-humanitarian*

moralism (properly oriented). On the one hand, there is concern for oneself and personal irresponsibility based on pure freedom; on the other, good feelings cultivated on the scale of society and the whole of humanity and agreeable to the egalitarian spirit of the age.

With respect to "personal morality," the golden rule is this: man is by nature innocent; he is emancipated from all moral responsibility, and so egoism is a good thing. Pure freedom consists in liberating oneself from any idea of the good, and how is this better expressed than in distancing oneself from the traditional version of the good? "Liberate yourself," the dominant discourse says, "reject taboos, think first of yourself and cultivate pleasures, especially those of a physical nature." In other words, the approved happiness consists in bodily well-being and in the pleasures of success. The favored way of living is to cultivate the idea of "each man for himself" and to strive constantly to acquire or preserve the most desirable goods, namely comfort, health, youth, "liberated" sexuality, entertainment, and the other signs of success. The official policy of tolerance does not require that one weigh traditional virtues and modern "virtues" equally in the balance.

Scientistic science is in the same camp. It works toward the technical mastery of the world and toward a purely material well-being while claiming a false neutrality that abolishes critical reflection. The science of economics in particular puts all of its knowledge and power in the service of the new "values": it gives voice to the social virtues of egoism, and it defines consumption as the ultimate good. Scientistic reason agrees with the materialist commandment: to live is to have.

This call for practical egoism goes hand-in-hand with an invasive social moralism. Giving in to one's appetites is considered good, but at the same time, nurturing grand sentiments is required. The misfortunes of those near to us matter little, but the misfortunes of the world require a vigilant eye and a bleeding heart. Here relativism gives way completely in order to give place to certain moral imperatives: the denunciation of evil and compassion for suffering humanity. In the moral world of Christianity, evil takes a thousand forms and penetrates every heart. In the new moral world, evil is clearly circumscribed; it is compressed, it is wholly embodied in a few attitudes, those which violate the new "values": racism, sexism, elitism, and all offenses against the ideology of human rights. The dominant discourse rejects ex cathedra the idea of sin, but in fact it reassigns the old religious roles: the world is divided into mortal sins on the one hand, and pure and perfect innocence on the other. Whoever holds the right opinion is ipso facto on the side of the just.[5]

This accusatory moralism is also a compassionate moralism. The dominant discourse, that of the masters of the word, trembles with emotion in confronting the misfortunes of the world. The victims' cries echo in the voices of opinion leaders. Compassion is one of the required sentiments, as long as it takes the approved form. First, this compassion must be directed less toward those who are close than those who are far away. The love of humanity is not about the family or neighborhood; it applies to the anonymous victims of "exclusion," "discrimination," "persecution," as well as to those of natural disasters. As a result, to display and preach this lovely senti- ment in public costs hardly anything: love is freed from the burdens of love; it demands little more than an emotion, a gesture, not true commitment. (Here we are speaking of those who do no more than talk, not of those who really give of themselves, preferably far from cameras.) Second, this compassion is directed solely toward man's physical nature; it scrupulously ignores moral conduct. Fashionable opinion hardly distinguishes, among the poor, between the aban- doned mother of a family and the professional parasite. The point is to do good without imposing an idea of the good. Finally, these victims are never those victims of the practical egoism justified by pure freedom. When there are guilty parties to be found, it must be those who violate the new "values": the wicked (real or supposed) who commit sins of racism, sexism, etc., and the institutions (in particular the family and the Church) that restrain pure freedom. Thus children who are victims of behaviors that discredit the family are considered worthy of interest, but children who are victims of behaviors that point up the crisis of the family hardly deserve attention. Once again two sets of standards are in play.[6]

In sum, the dominant discourse preaches not only the utter condemnation of the wicked, but also an egoistic self-love and an altruistic love of humanity. More precisely: self-love understood primarily as the search for immediate pleasure, and love of humanity understood as compassion for worthy cases of suffering. On the one hand, the reign of sensations; on the other, the morality of emotion. (The prevailing tone in films and on television is evidence of this: it oscillates between brutality and sentimentality, or else it combines the two.) In either case, reason is conspicuous by its absence.

3. *Appeal to modern historicism and "democratic" opinion.* Dominant opinion rests on two other arguments in enjoining each and all to rally to its cause, a historicist argument and a "democratic" argument. Its spokespersons say something like this: "This is the modern opinion—and how could you refuse to be of your era, to be in tune with your times? This is the general opinion—and how could you think that most people are wrong?" In both cases, the fundamental question is abolished and any discussion is superfluous. These arguments are injunctions to submit to the present because it is the present, and to the ruling and ostensibly general opinion because it is general; they are injunctions to submit to authorities other than reason. In a word, these are injunctions to abdicate all freedom of mind.

Modernity possesses a great power: it considers itself superior to all past worlds. In modern times, *modern* is a term of praise. How can one not be "modern"? It is understood that with time things go forward in every area, that this progress has all the signs of what is ineluctable, and that, consequently, a proper human being cannot help but be in touch with his times. Likewise, whoever refuses allegiance and opposes the dominant opinion can expect to be characterized in the required terms: his ideas are "archaic," "obsolete," "retrograde," or "conservative." Historicist rhetoric allows an argument to be dismissed without having to refute it. Discussion is pointless; history has settled everything: the right-thinking are presumed to be avant-garde, and those who think in the wrong way are considered to be fighting a rear-guard action. The experience of the twentieth century has not been sufficient to discredit this procedure.

If the dominant opinion exults in being modern; it also claims to express the general opinion. To a large degree, the dominant discourse presents itself as the mouthpiece of common opinion; it applies the pressure of the supposed opinion of the majority upon each individual: "Do things the right way, be like everyone else." Media personalities present new behavioral norms as normal, commonplace, almost natural; they present themselves as representatives of opinion, on the basis of surveys. (In fact, the game is largely controlled by the spokespeople, and not by those on whose behalf they are supposed to be speaking. In addition to the fact that their opinions are often manufactured, those who participate in polls have no power over the subject of the survey, the formulation of questions, the coding of responses, the interpretation of the numbers, or the significance attached to the results.) Throughout the discourse that rules the airwaves, it is society as a whole that seems to be speaking:

> Everything that is massively disseminated in the media seems massively to constitute the age, whether it is a matter of anonymous opinions, "progressive" morals, or new modes of existence. It is sufficient that the same images, the same ways of talking, the same ways of living become commonplace or banal in the domain of the media in order for the public to receive them immediately as ascendant "in today's world" and thus as obligatory. This is as true of the clothes we wear as of our economic vocabulary or the clichés of an interview or the conduct of a celebrity. Banalization is the current form of normativity.[7]

This norm, presented as commonplace and unproblematic, and thus legitimate and appropriate, is largely fabricated by those who give voice to the dominant discourse and those who inspire them. In other words, dominant opinion is not the same as the common opinion it claims to embody; it tends to shape it from the outside. It is not ordinary people who forged the new standards of good and evil and who orchestrated it through the media and to a large degree through the schools. Who can deny the key role of a minority of the population in the moral revolution that began in the sixties? The progress of equality by default is first and foremost the work of activists of equality by default: philosophers of unconditional freedom, critical theorists, immoderate advocates of human rights, radical feminists, extreme antiracist militants. At each stage, following a classic process, the movement progresses under the pressure of the most extreme activists, who themselves are surpassed at the next stage. This is the logic of radicalization: pure freedom always has more ground to conquer, and moral equality has more Bastilles to seize. The new principles undermine all resistance; as long as they are in place, the movement is irreversible, and it must go forward. By what right might one oppose it? If pure freedom is an unconditional good, then how can one answer those who argue for the free use of drugs or the right to euthanasia? If—as equality dictates—natural differences have no meaning, then why not extend all the rights of adults first to adolescents and then to children? If all personal choices are equal, then by what right refuse marriage to homosexuals? If every individual or every human group has its own "values," then what objection could be made to those who reject any universal norm of education? If all victims are by nature innocent, then what is there to say to those who abuse the status of victim? Every agent of modernity will find another modern who surpasses him, and every egalitarian will find another egalitarian who goes further than he does. The direction is set, and it is always possible to go further, up to the point of putting in question the cause of freedom itself in the name of radical equality or pure freedom.

Here again, opinions are unequal. The opinions of activists who play the tune of new "values" have power far beyond their numbers. The sympathy or acquiescence of those who control the media plays a large role here, the milieu in which they live being largely in the camp of ideas held to be "modern," a milieu very sensitive to positions and claims that tend in the right direction. The machine occupies a strategic position in the service of equality by default: its logic flattens the world, and its agents orchestrate the dominant "values." The result is that public or dominant opinion does not emanate or hardly emanates from the people; it is first of all the work of an avant-garde. More precisely, it results from the radicalization of modern thought, from the action of the militants of equality by default, from the strategic role of the masters of the electronic word.[8]

4

Dominant opinion operates behind a mask. It displays a fictitious moral neutrality, and presents itself fictitiously as the common opinion. This maneuver allows it to appeal to the idea of autonomy while enclosing autonomy within the circle of appropriate opinion. The success of this process is undeniable: the hold of a certain way of seeing and thinking has the allure of a liberation, and the reign of autonomy is indistinguishable from the reign of authorized opinion. Young people in particular are taken in by it; they have great difficulty believing in the possibility of a free mind thinking otherwise. They believe themselves to be autonomous, and they are conditioned.

They are conditioned to a way of seeing and thinking that flattens and debases life. For the Greeks, life was a tragedy and for the Christians, a drama. For the moderns led astray by ideology, life was a melodrama (the happy ending guaranteed). For the moderns of late modernity, life is no more than a trivial TV series. Dominant opinion invites us to lead a way of life that Tocqueville dreaded when he saw forming on the horizon "an innumerable crowd of men alike and equal whose lives revolve around themselves without respite in order to procure the little and vulgar pleasures with which they stuff their souls." The discourse of late modernity is not addressed to free people: "Be a master, yes, but a domesticated master."

CHAPTER 17
THE SELF AGAINST BEING

1

Imagine a discussion among moderns. They begin by discussing technical issues, but then the discussion takes a new turn. Now they are speaking more generally of issues with a bearing on private life— divorce, for example, or sexuality or leisure. The tone has hardly changed (it remains that of discussion, and not the more relaxed one of conversation), and yet this talking together no longer bears the marks of a true discussion (an exchange, some differences, some progression of ideas). What is being said is of another nature: a succession of separate opinions that are juxtaposed without ever contradicting each other because by definition they are all equally valid. Expressions such as "in my view," "to my way of thinking," and "in my opinion" are on everyone's lips; if anyone makes the mistake of presenting a proposition as true in itself and independent of opinion, he is immediately called to order: "That's what you say. It depends on one's point of view." Each person expresses his subjectivity and speaks only for himself as a fully autonomous individual, that is, an individual without tradition, without roots in a community, and without philosophic or religious allegiance. Everyone speaks, everyone participates without participating; no one really hears anyone else. And yet, in the absence of all dialogue, a certain tension prevails. This is not, to be sure, the tension of thought in search of truth, but a tension resulting from the will of each individual to affirm himself. If you are half-listening, you would take these to be personal opinions, but if you listen carefully, you would hear the echo of received opinion and, behind it, the echo of "me, myself, and I." The opinions themselves have little importance, but expressing them—and in so doing, expressing the idea that one is the creator of one's own law—is very important.

Then, at a given moment, for whatever reason, the tone changes. The masks begin to crack, the artifices give way; one person admits that he is uncertain and ill at ease, another speaks sincerely of something he admires, and everyone becomes more attentive to the others. An exchange takes place. A little later, under the influence of some unknown grace, the dimension of role-playing fades away completely, the interlocutors abandon all self-indulgence, and they speak with open hearts and engage themselves deeply in what they are saying. All find themselves on an equal footing, and each person senses the substantial community that ties him to the others. The atmosphere takes on a new density, a feeling of communion takes shape, everyone feels a heightened sense of being; an encounter takes place. What happens has nothing to do with an emotional fervor in which reason is abolished; what happens is a moment of joy in which reason is a full participant: it grasps the truth of human relations. This truth is established on the ruins of the Self. An encounter happens because each person has been disencumbered of his Self, because each one, in rediscovering his bonds with others, has recovered a bond with his being and with his inner freedom.

What was going on when each interlocutor spoke as an autonomous person to other autonomous people? No one was authentic. Each person remained a stranger to himself for two connected reasons that only seem to be in opposition: (1) each one was cut off from others, and (2) at the same time each one was alienated by others. The first reason is in keeping with what Gabriel Marcel explained and illustrated admirably: "The more my interlocutor is external, the more I am for that very reason external to myself."[1] It is only in a living relationship in which the other ceases to be a stranger that my external defenses crumble, that concern for self-image gives way, and that I achieve authenticity. As long as the relationship is distant and impersonal, I am not really, or I am only superficially, who I am. I am even less myself when—and this is the second reason—I put myself under someone else's control in complying with the obligation to take myself for my own master. In the above conversation, when the will to autonomy was dominant each person distanced himself from others and at the same time surrendered to their power. Each person wanted to be as autonomous as the others in relation to the others; each wanted to be autonomous, as everyone else was presumed to be, in order to make the right impression. Default man is similar to Dostoyevsky's underground man: he knocks himself out trying to show others he does not need them.

Grace has entered in. Now everything has changed. Each person feels liberated, each experiences this deliverance procured by self-renunciation: my self-love is quieted, I am freed of concern for the Self, I no longer look for myself in the looks of others, I become more what I am, I gain access to inner freedom. I gain access to inner freedom because I renounce pure freedom, this arbitrary freedom that is the lowest degree of freedom, because I adhere to a dedicated and ordered freedom that answers to the requirements of my being. I feel in harmony with myself because I give myself without hesitation and because truth is in command. If I allow myself the freedom to lie, then I immediately lose this feeling of liberation. I am truly free only when I am no longer master. *Inner freedom is the effacing of the self and the engaging of being.*

In this blessed moment, the feeling of liberation goes hand-in-hand with the feeling of fraternity. What all men have in common speaks to us: each person feels that all are made of the same stuff and embarked on the same boat; each experiences this fundamental human equality which consists in our common humanity. Equality and fraternity have often been presented as opposed to one another. But it is not equality in all its forms that is the enemy of fraternity, it is equality by default. Substantive equality, on the other hand, brings men together.

2

Imagine one of the individuals who took part in the discussion that took such a strange turn. When it comes time for him to take leave of the others, to whom he now feels much closer, he experiences a feeling he has never experienced before: a sense of fullness and freedom associated with inner peace. But this state of grace does not last. He is caught up again in what he takes for life; he once again enters the skin of modern man, addicted to abstractions and sensations. In a word, he returns to his prison: subjected to the dispersion of his Self, living his private life moment to moment in the name of sincerity, delivered over to the anarchy of his desires in the name of pure freedom, running from one "diversion" to another and glorying in his apparent autonomy. Once he tried bungee jumping. "It's a new sensation," he said. But bungee jumping does not satisfy him, no more than do other diversions. He is condemned to wander from one desired object to another, one moment of excitement to another, the Self always desiring and the heart desperately empty.

Unless . . . suppose the man in question has an adolescent son. He provides generously for his material well-being but otherwise leaves his son to himself with no more guidance than a "live your life," in which approach he sees proof of his "openness" and "tolerance." One day the house is empty. A note is left in plain view: "You never give anything! I'm out of here." The father is seized with anger: "What an ingrate! I leave him free; he has never lacked for anything, and look how he treats me!" But suddenly a verse from *Cinna* resonates in his memory: "Enter into yourself, Octavius, and cease to complain." The man gathers himself; he makes the necessary phone calls, then returns to his son's bedroom, this room filled up with his absence, and he does what he never does, he withdraws into himself and communes with himself. In this way he relieves himself of his Self, he puts it at a distance, he puts it in question, and he reaches a deeper part of himself. "Have I acted well?" he asks himself, "Have I done what was necessary?" By this very question, he brings about a conversion: he is no longer the master, no longer one who makes his own laws; he obeys requirements imposed on him. The more he detaches himself from his Self, the deeper he descends into the degrees of being, the more he achieves an inward unity in submitting himself to what is. This inner journey is a revelation. Within him now speaks an unknown faculty of reason, not the limited and subordinate reason he is accustomed to using, but a superior reason in which all his faculties collaborate: "My son is right. I have betrayed and abandoned him. I have rejected the duty that his very existence implied, and I have not answered his calls. I see very well why: I refused to let my responsibilities limit my freedom and I have not been willing to love fully, because love is a commitment and a form of dependence. At bottom, what is my life but a perpetual refusal to love? The modern man that I am is first and foremost *the man who refuses to give himself.* The freedom on which I pride myself makes me deaf, unavailable, irresponsible; the Self that governs me cuts off all the movements of being. The truth is that I have not lived. The truth is that I am not this life, that I am other than these acts. It is time that I put myself in harmony with who I am, with what is; it is time to do what I must, and first of all to make amends with my son." The man feels a burden lifting; he is disencumbered of himself, finally free. He has consented, he has chosen to no longer have a choice, he is liberated.

What happened next? Did he get back his son? How far did he go in self-effacement and in the engagement of being, in self-effacement and the reception of being? The story does not say. What is certain is that he never again went bungee jumping.

3

The modern self, the Self with a capital S, is, one might say, an absolute self. It is based on the ordinary self but it has its own orientation. The ordinary self is the disposition that leads a person to relate everything to himself; in other words, it is indistinguishable from an egocentrism as old as the world. The modern self is a radical egocentrism that no doubt owes something to ordinary egocentrism or concern for oneself but that results first of all from the imperative that, as we have seen, characterizes late modernity: be yourself, be fully autonomous. The modern self is absolute because it stands upon the ruins of the objective world. But nature is not violated with impunity: so understood, the Self cannot be grasped. What is this *ego* that is supposed to govern life and that has no cause, no ends, and belongs to no community (neither son of his father, nor native of his land), that has no relation with the nature of things? What is this singular self that is dependent on no one and nothing? The Self is dispersed, divided, disordered. Modern man abdicates all internal coherence. His destiny is to never find himself, to run ceaselessly after an ever-uncertain identity, after expressions of the Self that distinguish it from others and after the recognition of others. The Self is never sufficient unto itself; it needs external support. But every other human being is also a Self. In the world of autonomy, each Self shows off in front of the others.

Jean-Jacques Rousseau set things in motion. With all the resources of his genius, he gave the contradictions of the Self a wonderful and pathetic form: he claimed his innocence in the name of his conscience, the only tribunal he recognized. And he pled his case tirelessly before others: he claimed to be self-sufficient and never stopped proclaiming it before the world. Rousseau is an avant-garde thinker; he urged everyone to lose himself as he had, in this desert haunted by others to which the tyranny of the Self leads.

4

There are ways of being that are also degrees of being. Is it necessary to give multiple examples? I am not the same, in being or degree of being, when I admire as compared with when I belittle, when I forgive as when I stay hardened in resentment, when I strain toward truth as when I am riddled with vanity, when I am wholly involved in a common undertaking as when I am turned inward on my own interests, when I am penetrated by love of those close to me as when I abandon myself to lust, when I give myself as when I refuse myself. The more I forget myself and commit my being, the more I am; the more I rise above my inner division in favor of what is deepest in me, the more I am. The egocentrism of the self, and even more the radical egocentrism of the modern self, debases and spoils life. It blocks what nourishes the human heart. What are moments of joy if not those in which the self is silent? These are the moments when being resonates, breathes, swells in the accomplishment of a task well done, the admiration of works of genius, wonder before beauty, collaboration in a common enterprise, an encounter steeped in friendship, being carried away by love. Contrary to what late modernity says, true authenticity is achieved by conquering the self. But the conquest is difficult, always to be renewed and always incomplete. The self is a tireless seducer and its ruses are infinite, as the French moralists of the seventeenth century have said so superbly. To be inwardly torn is our fate. Everything happens, as Bergson says, as if there were in man an original defect of workmanship.

Is there any need to name all the philosophers and writers who have come to the same conclusion?[1] The preceding discussions are only variations on a theme treated, illustrated, illuminated a thousand times in different ways in the framework of Christian thought and elsewhere. Let it suffice to cite Saint Augustine's *Confessions*, Pascal's critique of the self, Newman's distinction between the self and the ground of being, Bergson's concept of spiritual energy, Gabriel Marcel's analyses of the self and the I . . . and the whole line of writers that stretches from Dante to Solzhenitsyn and includes Dostoyevsky, Péguy, and Bernanos.[2] The crux is always found at the same point: the self is a barrier, a block. To see, to commune, one must get over the self.

5

To see and to enable others to see is everything. Vital reason does not begin by constructing, calculating, aligning propositions, lining up reasons; what is first and foremost in vital reason is the ability to see things clearly. And to see clearly, one must look, and look in the right way; in other words, one must employ one's vital reason. How then is this defined? What is called *vital reason*, in its highest form, is of the realm of higher reason as described in different forms by Saint Thomas (the *intellectus*), Pascal (the *heart*), Bergson (*intuition*); it is reason that apprehends its object directly. In other words, what is proper to higher reason comes down to this: as far as it is able, it grasps truth in the form of *self-evidence*. It sees, and the truth is so compelling that it leaves no room for doubt; it remains to reason only to bow before it. Only self-evidence, as we have seen, makes it possible to know that two is not one, that two and two are four, or that the external world exists. Self-evidence is at the origin of all knowledge and it belongs to the realm of the highest form of knowledge. If our higher reason could be applied universally, we would need neither concepts nor chains of reasoning. It was Saint Thomas, himself a master of the art of reasoning, who said that "reasoning is a defect of intelligence (*intellectus*)."

In its realm, vital reason thus operates first by grasping what is evident. The truths it apprehends do not lend themselves to proof; they are immediately recognized as truths. Here, higher reason does not limit itself to primary evidences or to the evidence of the validity of the conclusions of reasoning reason; it explores, it digs deeper, it expands its faculty of vision, it broadens and deepens the field of evidence. The great visionaries (artists, philosophers, spiritual leaders) are those who see farther than we do and who invite us to follow them. The truths they bring to light cannot be shared in the way that a scientific discovery is shared. Each person must make his own way, he must rediscover for himself. The great visionaries are witnesses; they enable us to see truths, they invite us to share the same inner experience, to find for ourselves the truths to which they testify. These are truths that are compelling not because they give rise to a fleeting emotion but because they are in harmony with the constitution of our being, because they are recognized as being consubstantial with who we are. It is no accident if one of the criteria of good discernment is the heart's profound peace.[3]

To see this, one must want and give oneself the means to see it. The exercise of vital reason presupposes an attitude toward the world that is opposite to the one implied by scientistic reason. The latter results from a dissociation of human faculties that works to the detriment of being and the benefit of the Self. For scientistic reason, to think is to think with just a part of oneself, with that part that allows one, with the help of method, to dominate an object. To think is to look down from on high and thus to affirm oneself; at the limit it means to apply one's pride to the debasement of one's object. By contrast, vital reason presupposes a unifying of faculties to the detriment of the Self. To think is to commit one's whole being and to efface oneself before the object. To think is to be available, receptive, to let oneself be taken up by the truth. Vital reason is inseparable from the virtues of understanding and in the first instance from humility before what is real.

It follows that vital reason is more or less at work or more or less on the back burner in different people and in different periods. In the history of the West, it was actualized and progressed thanks to classical philosophy and Christian thought. Today, it is obscured and hampered by late modernity: the Self prevents us from seeing beyond the Self. Moreover the reigning relativism tends to disqualify it: "What is the validity of evidence that is not evident for everyone? How can this so-called superior reason be valid in the face of the extreme diversity of manners and customs? There is no universal morality. The only universal viewpoint is that of science, and science puts all other claims to universality in their true place: as the expression of a 'culture' or of one subjectivity among so many others." This objection is commonplace, but it still contradicts itself and contradicts other common and dominant opinions: if the multiplicity and the variety of "cultures" is sufficient to give the lie to all human universality, then science too must abdicate its pretensions to universality, the universality of the rights of man must be seen as a fiction, and the vaunted superiority of the modern world must be admitted to be without foundation. But the internal contradictions of late modernity are not sufficient to get beyond it. To remove the objection in question, two other arguments must be advanced.

The first is this: vital reason is without any doubt very unequally actualized in different historical conditions and in different subjects, but the fact that it is present everywhere is attested in a thousand ways: what human group among all those that have been studied is without any rule of morality? What morality among all those that are known has ever preached murder, theft, rape, incest, sacrilege, lying? What society has ever established arbitrariness of punishment as a principle? What tyrant ever proclaimed his pleasure in tyrannizing? What torturer ever boasted of the intrinsic merits of torture? Why is the thief shocked when someone steals from him? Why is the scientist wounded when someone questions his intellectual honesty? Why, as James Q. Wilson notes, is crime actually so rare? Why, in the example so dear to Jean Piaget, do children playing marbles spontaneously reproach the cheater?[4]

This first claim is, of course, insufficient. The diversity of laws and of mores springs from a common core, but it is still vast.[5] Another essential reflection must be added: contrary to what is postulated by the dominant way of thinking (whether it is a question of egalitarian doctrine or scientism), the universal is not reducible to the general. The proposition "the sequence of numbers is infinite" is a universally valid evidence of arithmetic even though multitudes of people have never known anything of it; the proposition "space has three dimensions" is a self-evident principle of geometry even though it has never occurred to many people. What is the significance of these examples borrowed from Pascal? They attest to the fact that there are self-evident truths not evident to everyone. The same is true of the profound truths of life or being: they are the achievements of vital reason; they must be discovered or rediscovered; they have a history even if, unlike the truths of mathematics, they can be lost or fall into obscurity. To elevate the general to the status of the universal is to put barbarous practices and civilized mores on the same level; it is to give the same standing to the blind, the myopic, and the sighted. When cannibals eat their enemy, when peoples practice slavery, what does this show except their inability to see that the other belongs to the same humanity? When the Nazis divided human beings into masters and subhumans, what did they demonstrate if not a regression in vital understanding? When the mathematician Roberval cries out upon leaving a performance of Corneille's *Polyeucte*, "What does that prove?" what does this say except to point up his limitation as a man imprisoned in science? When a brutal person is untouched by a sublime spectacle, what does it bring to light besides his brutality? On the other hand, Socrates, Michelangelo, Pascal, Rembrandt, Bach, Solzhenitsyn, and others bear witness for all human beings because they "see" farther than we do. "The universal," Gabriel Marcel writes, "is located in the dimension of personal depth, and not at all in that of extension. The most personal works are those that are richest in universal significance."[6] This is so because the most profoundly personal works are also those in which the Self is effaced and no longer presents an obstacle.

6

The modern world, according to Bernanos, is a vast conspiracy against the inner life. Is it necessary to recapitulate all the formidable means this conspiracy has at its disposal to cut man off from his being and to enclose him within his Self, to dispossess him of his vital reason, and finally to alienate him? Those means include everything that blocks out the substance of life: a dominating knowledge that obscures the world and shackles the mind and the spirit, an information machine that produces a deafening and meaningless din. Those means also include everything that invites modern man to be satisfied with his condition: the illusion of autonomy without the burden of liberty, the seduction of entertainment and the temptations of intemperance, the dismissal of any feeling that entails obligation, first of all respect and love. Modern man is liberated from that which has the power to liberate him from himself. He is imprisoned in a cave that glows with a thousand lights; he feels fine there and does not want to be bothered. The great success of late modernity is that it produces that form of slavery which Vauvenargues described as a slavery that "abases human beings to the point of making itself loved for doing it."

And yet there is more. This world has a great power of conditioning and seduction, but it is incapable of fulfilling man's being. What can it promise except always to go in the same direction? Thus there arises a feeling of disenchantment and malaise, as shown for example in the pervasiveness of subrational beliefs (when one loses faith in God, the danger, as Chesterton said, is not that one no longer believes in anything but rather that one will believe anything). Are not the human beings of late modernity deep within themselves more or less troubled by a soft voice that says: this cannot be what it means to live, can it? Modern man is not irrevocably the last man. History is not finished.

EPILOGUES

EPILOGUE 1

1

Liberal modernity has brought about extraordinary progress, progress without precedent in the history of humanity, and yet it issues in a failure: the promise of emancipation has not been kept; worse, it turns out to be a fool's bargain. Supposedly grownup men and women think and live as they are told to think and live: with a fraction of themselves, beneath themselves. There is one and only one fundamental reason for this failure: a false idea of human emancipation. Modernity has given in to its subjectivist tendency. In other words, people have become full of themselves, they have become giddy. The heavens are empty, nature is mute, man is at last free and sovereign; he enjoys an original innocence, his will is the rule of things, he has the power to create himself and to subjugate the world, the day of the regnum hominis has truly begun. From this there results the following paradoxical fact: the modern world was in its origins more natural than earlier worlds, yet it gradually cut all its ties to nature. Modern hubris has spoiled everything.

2

This subjectivist ferment lies at the heart of the whole modern venture. It is what has caused liberal modernity to spin out of control, and it is even more at work in the other, ideological, version of modernity. Why has the power of ideology had this extraordinary capacity to survive the radical failure of its promise of collective emancipation? There is no mystery in this. The ideological formula liberates and exalts the role of the will in history and confers all rights upon it—in the name of The Cause, everything is permitted. The ideological revolution is the work of a will that becomes intoxicated with its power, a will that imposes itself and denies the resistance of nature and ends in a fictional universe. What, after all, was communist totalitarianism? The apotheosis of subjectivism. In the world of "utopia made real" (Alain Besançon), reality no longer has its own substance; it is whatever the Party says it is. Truth is without any value, as O'Brien explains to Winston Smith in the basement of the Ministry of Love; what matters, the only thing that matters, is power. On the ruins of meaning, only one thing remains: the will of the masters.

3

Two versions of subjectivism, two promises of emancipation (individual and collective), two failures. But if these two failures have a common root, they are not of the same nature. However deserving of criticism late modernity may be, it is a haven of peace, sweetness, and liberty compared with the world of Orwell. The failure of ideology is a radical failure, a failure that condemns absolutely any claim to hold the keys of universal redemption and therefore to construct the kingdom of righteousness on earth. The shipwreck took everything with it. There are no good seeds to be saved. The radical-liberal failure, on the other hand, does not discredit the original principle—only the extreme form it has taken; it does not discredit the ideas of universal equality and personal liberty but rather their corrupt versions, equality by default and pure freedom. Here, it is necessary to distinguish the wheat from the tare.

Originally, as we have seen, the good seed was mixed with tare. The good seed is the idea of the worth and dignity of every human being as a human being, a being at once singular, unique, irreplaceable, and fully a member of the same humanity. The tare is the subjectivism that has progressively taken over and tends to invade everything: the human person is effaced in favor of default man. Throughout the course of this evolution, this derailment, the classical and Christian soil has been exhausted, in a way. Babylon prospers on the ruins of Athens and of Jerusalem.

It follows that liberal principles, insofar as they are formal principles, are not self-sufficient. The modern world (liberal version) is incapable of staying the course of itself without derailing; it needs a substance from elsewhere; it needs a substance that maintains, nourishes, and elevates the ideas of equality and of liberty and opens onto what lies beyond our understanding. If the desert is expanding, it is because the two wellsprings of Western civilization have dried up: Greek philosophy and Christianity.

4

Is the horizon closed? This world, which exalts man's free will, is the same one that says: there is nothing to do but what we are doing; the future is laid out in advance, even if we who are shaping it are groping in the dark. History is no longer a promise, but it is still a constraint. Yet the choice exists, a choice that presents itself fundamentally in the same terms defined by Tocqueville at the end of *Democracy in America*: either one must accommodate oneself to a modern world that is becoming less and less civilized, that is miserably digging itself a deeper and deeper hole, that is transforming itself imperceptibly into what Milan Kundera calls the "collectivity of the stupefied"; or one must work to contain this drift, and, beyond this, one must lift up this world by renewing its ties with its great heritage. From this point of view, politics is only one means of action among others, but it is a necessary means. Only public action is capable of checking or subordinating modern economic and technical logic, which advances powerfully without knowing where it is going. Only public action can discipline our information and entertainment machine, which is becoming more and more a machine of distortion and degradation. But such would require that politics be restored to its vocation—to take responsibility for the common interest—and that it put itself in the service of the truth regarding what man is. What is needed are statesmen.

5

"Politics in the service of the truth about man!" modern man objects one last time. "Have you understood nothing, have you learned nothing from the experiences of the twentieth century, from the totalitarian experiences you yourself have talked about? In politics truth kills or at best oppresses. Our world is the best of all possible worlds. Are you an ideologue in disguise?" We can agree that any approach to politics the purpose of which is something other than the freedom of individuals carries with it certain risks of derailment, even if it is founded on correct ideas. Does it follow that politics must abdicate? The solution, it seems to us, is the following: politics must walk a fine line between two temptations. On the one hand, it must not give in to the exaltation of political will; on the other, it must not abandon the future of our civilization to a runaway logic and to the activists of equality by default. More precisely, to walk this fine line is to respect two key rules that radically distinguish realist from ideological politics.

1. Realist politics is devoted to the ongoing effort by trial and error to find points of equilibrium. The social world is not that of all or nothing, as the ideologue believes; it is one in which social purposes oppose and limit each other. The difficulty consists in "seeing double" (Maurice Blondel), in holding on to both ends of the chain, in considering at once what is owing to substantive equality and what is owing to inequalities of merit and talent, what is owing to freedom and what is a matter of intolerable uses of freedom, what technology and the market provide and what they destroy, what is within the domain of individual liberty and what are the obligations of the citizen or the parent. Contrary to what is

suggested by the "categorical" language of the rights of man, the tension between desirable and competing purposes is inherent in social life. There is no pure solution.

2. Realist politics is destined to be always pursuing, always starting over again, never coming to an end. There is no complete solution. Ideologues have claimed to tear up the roots of evil by changing political and social conditions. In this they could only fail: evil resides in the heart of each human being. In *The Diary of a Country Priest* by Georges Bernanos, the priest of Torcy tells this story: a good sister of Bruges who served in the parish had declared war on dust. She did not only want to fight it, which made sense; she wanted to make it disappear once and for all. The good sister died in this effort, but the dust remained. Everything must always begin again.

6

Everything must always begin again in politics and beyond. Everything must begin again on new foundations and on the same foundations. The modern world, despite its claims, has changed nothing in the metaphysical condition of man. Human beings live on this earth in a state of want. So what do serious people propose other than to share their incurable frivolity?

> Et ce ne sera pas ces frêles greluchons
> qui nous adorneront le jour du jugement
> Et ce ne sera pas ces savants petits maîtres
> Qui nous équiperont le jour du tremblement.
>
> Et ce ne sera pas ces savants petits maîtres
> qui nous adorneront le jour du jugement
> Et ce ne sera pas ces lamentables êtres
> qui nous équiperont le jour du tremblement.
>
> Et ce ne sera pas leurs illustres travaux
> Qui nous adorneront le jour de la colère

Et ce ne sera pas ces poneys et ces veaux
Le jour du dernier prix et du dernier salaire.

. . . .

Et nous ne fierons rien qu'aux voiles de prière
Parce que c'est Jésus qui nous les a tissées
Et nous ne fierons rien qu'aux voiles de misère
Parce que c'est Jésus qui nous les a hissées."[1]

EPILOGUE 2

NON

The following letter came into our hands in ways that, the reader will understand, cannot be revealed. Suffice it to say that a copy was found in the American or European offices of Mephistopheles, accompanied by a list of addressees. It was stamped with the word "confidential" and carried with it a strong odor of sulfur. Here is the complete text:

> Henceforth I know you well enough, my dear associate, to know that you do not belong to the craven herd, that you belong among those whom nothing can intimidate. You are worthy of being counted among the elect. I am going to tell you the secret of freedom. You know how the masses are to be addressed. I make them believe that freedom is beyond good and evil, that there is no harm in doing evil. I have no complaint about the results. These fools do what is expected: a lot of little modern sins, of the kind that corrupt manners and morals and unravel society. There is no other way with this kind of people; one has to use trickery, or they become frightened. These are the timid, the pusillanimous, and the petty sinners; when one tells them "the sea is free," they

paddle along the shore. At bottom they are delighted to have buoys placed along their route, to have the burden of their freedom removed. By themselves they are incapable of taking seriously the idea that "all is permitted."

You deserve better; you deserve to be included in the few who know. Pay attention, for I am going to confide the secret to you: true freedom is not beyond good and evil; it is in evil chosen for its own sake. Be wicked, deliberately wicked, intensely wicked, and I promise you the pleasures of a king. One only savors one's freedom, one's power, one's might in an action that is wrong and that is known to be wrong. The ones who do good are inferior beings. Understand this well: to do good is to get on one's knees, to subjugate oneself, to give up. True freedom lies in transgression willed for its own sake. That is why I urge you to lie wantonly: as a matter of principle and constantly. The semi-skilled, the naughty little ones lie out of self-interest or boastfully, for petty reasons. They have understood nothing. The lie as lie is part of the great art of living, the art of the strong. The truth—the old bitch—shackles the will; she is by nature an enemy. Believe me, dear associate, do as I do, lie for the sake of lying, do evil for the sake of evil. Only in this way will you get the upper hand on the world and stand up to God. Only in this way will you become a master.

I am telling you this because I know that you do not have the soul of a slave and that you can bear strong words. The great danger, the great temptation is to love. These stinking Christians with their soft virtues say, "Love is lovable." But I tell you in truth: love is hateful. If you love, you give in, you lose, you abase yourself. If you want to dominate, then detest. True freedom, the freedom of lords, is that of hatred—intense, extreme, absolute hatred. What pleasure, my friend, what exquisite delight when you crush a face beneath your boot or when you sully a pure soul. Heaven weeps, and you are king. Once you have tasted this drunkenness, you will realize just how insipid and wretched your former life was. In a word, I invite you to make your own the great maxim of rebellious angels and supermen: "Hate and do as you will."

I am sure that you will not back down and that I can henceforth count you among my faithful. And so I propose to have you participate in our great work of the moment. First, attack the children. Apply yourself to damaging them, debasing them, depraving them. As you know, we have already done some good work: no one any longer dares to speak of purity; no one dares to speak of perversions. The way has been cleared: choose what is ignoble and have a good time. Next, attack the only fortress that remains to be taken, that infamous Roman church that has for centuries contended for my kingdom. Round about, the work is already well under way, but the Roman papacy does not give in. No need for me to tell you the themes to orchestrate: the denunciation of prohibitions, of dogmatism, of what is archaic. *Delenda est Roma.*

Here as elsewhere, it goes without saying you must always work in disguise. Put yourself on the side of freedom, the rights of man, opposition to racism, and humanitarian sentiments alongside the simpletons who believe in all that crap. No one will see any malice in this; I have taught them to not see it. They no longer believe in evil, the idiots, after all that I have accomplished in the last century. They are as credulous as Orgon, so you can play Tartuffe with impunity. The way is clear for some magnificent deceptions.

As you see, I am confident. We shall succeed in ruining, in bringing down, in leveling this execrable civilization that has presented so many obstacles to our freedom. A new era is taking shape on the horizon, an era in which the last trace of the Crucified will have disappeared from this earth. Finally!

Be one of us. I am counting on you. You will rule with us over the rubble, and, I promise you, we will have a good laugh.

Is this letter authentic? The experts are undecided. If it is authentic, is the Evil One boasting? Who knows? What is certain is this: "Throughout the West, war has been declared on the Western Judeo-Christian heritage, and we are losing this war."[1] *Sursum Corda.*

NOTES

CHAPTER 1

1. Alexis de Tocqueville, *Democracy in America*, vol. 2, 3, 1. On this point, see Robert Legros, "La Reconnaissance sensible de l'homme par l'homme," *Epokhé*, no. 2 (1991): 237–62.
2. On the birth and development of modern thought, see in particular the works of Leo Strauss, especially *Natural Right and History* (Chicago: Univesity of Chicago Press, 1953) and *What Is Political Philosophy* (Glencoe, Ill.: Free Press, 1959), and Pierre Manent's *La Cité de l'homme* (Paris: Fayard, 1994).
3. Michel Villey, *Le Droit et les droits de l'homme* (Paris: Presses Universitaires de France [P.U.F.], 1983).
4. Manent, *La Cité de l'homme*, 199.

CHAPTER 2

1. Is it necessary to add that in practice Christian institutions, and first of all the Roman Church, have of course not always been in harmony with the Gospel teaching? The princes of the Church have not all been saints, and saints have often had their problems with the princes of the Church.
2. *The Merchant of Venice,* act 3, scene 1, lines 52–62.
3. G. K. Chesterton, *Heretics* (London: The Bodley Head, 1905), 275.
4. *Of the Law of Nature and Nations* (1740), bk. 3, pt. 2, ch. 1.

5. There is another reason *"touche pas à mon pote"* is not a formula of mutual respect. "We are all brothers" implies reciprocal obligations; the more casual formula posits a one-way relationship that implies obligations only for one party. Are obligations dependent on race? Are some exempt from what is required of others? The logic of this formulation leads to the following: racism is the attribute of a race; the racial criterion is valid once it is reversed. But to struggle against racism does not mean to give in to a misguided antiracism. (This analysis is developed in my "De la corruption de l'antiracisme," *Commentaire*, no. 37 [Spring 1987]: 116–21.)

6. See Part 3. Let us add a clarification of vocabulary: here and in what follows, we employ, for convenience, the expressions "modern man" or "modern equality" to designate late-modern equality and humanity, that is, humanity by default or equality by default.

CHAPTER 3

1. "I admit I don't much like negligence as concerns things," wrote the great professor Marc Bloch; "it easily carries over to the mind." *L'Étrange défaite. Témoignage écrit en 1940* (Paris: Gallimard, coll. Folio, 1992), 89.

2. Annie Kriegel, *Le Figaro* (12 September 1983).

CHAPTER 4

1. Tocqueville, *Democracy in America*, vol. 2, 3, 5.

2. I borrow this remark from Pierre Manent, *Tocqueville and the Nature of Democracy* (Lanham, Md.: Rowman & Littlefield, 1996).

3. Reported by Alain Finkielkraut, "Malaise dans la démocratie," *Le Débat*, no. 51 (September–October 1988): 131.

4. Jeanne Hersch, *Éclairer l'obscur* (Lausanne: L'ge d'Homme, 1986), 70–71.

5. Things are no doubt different in the material realm, that is, in the realm of having, since in modern societies the underprivileged enjoy a degree of protection without historical precedent. Social progress in this area is undeniable, even if it is mixed with unintended negative

side effects. But this "solidarity" works only through the interposition of a public agency; it neither represents nor creates strong social bonds.

6. Cited by Georges Liebert, "Le Mérite de Georges. Réponse," *Commentaire*, no. 72 (Winter 1995–96): 880.

CHAPTER 5

1. Here we leave aside contemporary epistemology, which pushes relativism so far as to put in question the idea of scientific truth, because among scientists and the general public it does not carry much weight against what common sense can see: science or technoscience "works"; its efficacy is extraordinary. (On the theses of contemporary epistemology, see in particular the magisterial presentation of Raymond Boudon in *L'Art de se persuader* [Paris: Fayard, 1990].) In other words, "hard" science remains on the whole faithful to these two attitudes: it is on the side of objectivity and it speaks in universal (or transcultural) terms. In this it limits relativism and subjectivism, which for us clearly counts in its favor.

2. Of course techniques can be useful, and in certain disciplines they are obviously necessary—as long as they always remain servants and do not dispense with more fundamental qualities. As Péguy wrote in his polemic against the "new Sorbonne": "One attributes to methods and to instruments—which have their importance, a certain importance, but a completely methodological and instrumental importance—a major importance, an importance so total that they must provide for everything. Thus one produces and launches into the world of higher education these little, artificial, skinny young men, who possess to one degree or another certain tools and methods, but who possess no content." ("De la situation faite à l'histoire et à la sociologie dans les temps modernes" [1906], in Péguy, *Oeuvres en prose complètes*, vol. 2 [Paris: Gallimard, 1988], 486–87.) François Furet echoes this thought in addressing our times: "One of the dramas of the 'social sciences' just about everywhere today consists in leading young scholars to believe that, by limiting themselves to the acquisition of

the mere techniques of 'scientific' analysis, they can do without any familiarity with the great authors" (*Le Monde* [19 May 1992]).

3. Irving Kristol, *Reflections of a Neoconservative* (New York: Basic Books, 1983), 304.

CHAPTER 6

1. Of little importance here are divisions between schools and different versions of the objective (these are so many variants of the same fundamental theme). In any case, we leave aside here those who strive to extend economic analysis to the whole of human activities. We will meet them a little further on.

2. Charles Péguy, *L'Argent* (1913), in *Oeuvres en prose complètes,* vol. 3 (Paris: Gallimard, 1992), 789–90.

3. Charles Péguy, *Personnalités* (5 April 1902), in *Oeuvres en prose complètes,* vol. 1 (Paris: Gallimard, 1987), 921.

4. Charles Péguy, *Cahiers de la Quinzaine* (posthumous) (1906), in *Oeuvres en prose complètes,* vol. 2 (Paris: Gallimard, 1988), 460.

5. Charles Péguy, *Clio* (1913), in *Oeuvres en prose complètes*, vol. 3, 1020, 1015.

6. Charles Péguy, *Note conjointe sur M. Descartes et la philosophie cartésienne* (1914), in *Oeuvres en prose complètes*, vol. 3, 456.

7. Good A is preferable to good B up to the point at which the utility of an additional unit of good A divided by its unit price becomes equal to the utility of an additional unit of good B divided by its unit price.

8. Charles Péguy, *Heureux les systématiques* (1906), in *Oeuvres en prose complètes,* vol. 2, 295–96.

9. The pioneers in this area are Anthony Downs, James Buchanan (Nobel Prize 1986), Gordon Tullock, and Gary Becker (Nobel Prize 1992). For an overall presentation of these theories, see especially Louis Lévy-Garboua, *Sociological Economics* (London: Sage, 1979); and Dennis Mueller, *Public Choice II* (Cambridge: Cambridge University Press, 1989).

10. This way of looking at human beings is obviously so reductionist as

to be absurd. Sensitive to this commonsensical critique, certain economists have given a broader definition of economic man and utility by including the possibility of "altruistic" behaviors. But then one of two things must follow: either altruism involves feelings, such as the charitable impulse of a Good Samaritan, opposed to egoistic calculation, and the concept of utility (or of *homo economicus*) is stretched so as to become a catch-all including behaviors by nature radically different (whoever applies the same concept to a thing and to its opposite empowers himself to explain everything by explaining nothing), or, on the other hand, altruism is not opposed to egoism, but is only a variant of it in which the advantages sought are simply of a different nature; thus, for example, a moral dilemma is only a particular form of calculation of interests. This latter interpretation is of course the one favored by our economists: altruism is only a form of egoism. So we are back on familiar ground.

11. [Trans.] Here is Corneille's famous original text (lines 1727–29):

> Je vois, je sais, je crois, je suis désabusée
> De ce bienheureux sang, tu me vois baptisée
> Je suis chrétienne enfin, n'est-ce pas assez dit?

> [I see, I know, I believe, I am disabused.
> Of this felicitous blood, you see that I am baptized.
> I am at last a Christian, does this not say enough?]

CHAPTER 7

1. [Trans.] This scene takes place at the beginning of Racine's tragedy *Andromaque* (1667), act 1, scene 4. After the fall of Troy, King Pyrrhus holds Andromache, the widow of Hector, and her son as prisoners. Pyrrhus loves Andromache, who does not reciprocate, but rather intends to remain faithful to Hector. The following translation cannot of course do justice to Racine's style:

> I was going to the place where they keep my son
> Since once a day you allow me to enjoy
> The sight of all I have left of Hector and of Troy.
> I was going, sir, to weep a moment with him,
> Yet today I have not been able to embrace him.

2. Allan Bloom, *The Closing of the American Mind* (New York: Simon & Schuster, 1987).

3. See Bloom, *The Closing of the American Mind,* part 2, chaps. 4, 5, and 6. It should be clear that this criticism does not extend to all the technical terms of sociology, but only to those which, by virtue of the method itself, crush vital differences. (And here we treat only those terms which have become current in public discourse.)

4. I should add that the influence of economists is spread by this vulgarization of economic categories much more than by the diffusion of economic reasoning. Economic reasoning is reasoning in terms of alternatives (every decision has an opportunity cost, that is, the benefits sacrificed because other possible uses of the same resources have to be forgone), of more and less (calculations at the margin), and of actions and reactions according to the logic of incentives. On the scope and limits of this style of reasoning, see especially Steven E. Rhoads, *The Economist's View of the World* (Cambridge: Cambridge University Press, 1985), pt. 1.

5. See the pioneering works of Raymond Boudon, especially *Effets pervers et ordre social* (Paris: P.U.F., 1977).

6. Has anyone ever taken determinism seriously to its limit? Who ever lived as if all freedom were denied him? Certainly not the apostles of determinism, who behave as if they had been declared exempt by some official mandate. Deterministic theories are always, it seems, in the service of something else: theoretical ambition ("I am the master of meaning"), voluntarism ("workers of the world, unite!"), irresponsibility ("society alone is guilty").

CHAPTER 8

1. All information on the history and system of McDonald's is borrowed from George Ritzer, *The McDonaldization of Society* (Newbury Park, Calif.: Pine Forge Press, 1993).

2. As a counterexample, let us cite the beautiful film by Gabriel Axel, *Babette's Feast*, based on a novel by Karen Blixen. In this film, a political exile from France (a *communarde* [a participant in the uprising that formed the Paris Commune of 1871]), who had been a great chef under the Second Empire, offers his Danish hosts a refined dinner in the French style. And what happens? The French arts of the table and gastronomy in effect liberate the Danes from their Puritan reserve; little by little the conversation becomes freer, old attitudes give way, human beings become warmer, and the guests discover something unknown to them, a moment of shared joy in which the pleasures of the creation bring creatures together.

CHAPTER 9

1. For more on this purely procedural conception of liberal democracy (as opposed to the substantive version of this same regime), see the following chapter.

2. Nathan Glazer, *The Limits of Social Policy* (Cambridge, Mass.: Harvard University Press, 1988), 154.

3. American feminism provides an extreme example: though it of course feels little sympathy for heterosexual marriage, its logic leads it to demand legal guarantees and a formal written contract prior to any amorous relations between a man and woman. As François Furet has written, "the idea of moral customs is rejected as reactionary in favor of the universal rule of legal abstractions, even in the household economy, in family life, in sexual relations. . . . Soon it will be necessary for the two partners to bring their lawyers in order to prepare the necessary documents before going to bed together—especially when one of them is rich and the other is not." ("L'utopie démocratique américaine," *Le Débat*, no. 69 (March–April 1992): 85–86.

4. For a detailed analysis of the new rights of the child and militant

advocacy for such rights in France, see Irène Théry, "Nouveaux droits de l'enfant, la potion magique?" *Esprit*, no.180 (March–April 1992): 5–30.

5. Aristotle, *Propos* (Paris: Éd. de la Pléiade, 1956), 925–26.

6. Alain Finkielkraut, "La Nouvelle statue de Pascal Morozov," *Le Monde* (9 January 1990).

CHAPTER 10

1. This example comes from Harvey Mansfield's "Responsibility versus Self-Expression," in *Old Rights and New*, ed. Robert A. Licht (Washington, D.C.: AEI Press, 1993), 96.

2. The following passage is directly inspired by Harvey Mansfield's *America's Constitutional Soul* (Baltimore: Johns Hopkins University Press, 1991).

3. Polling can be considered a democratic procedure only according to a purely procedural interpretation. From a substantive perspective, voting and polling are radically different for two reasons: (1) voting is not an unconditioned expression of any opinion whatever; it is a deliberate choice, subject to precise forms, situated in a certain context; and (2) voting (except in a referendum), unlike polling, concerns the selection of representatives, and representation itself involves the rationalization of democracy—although it is of course subject to corruption. On the practice of polling, see chapter 15.

CHAPTER 11

1. Here we will not attempt to resolve the difficult question of the respective roles of techno-technical and techno-economic rationality. Sometimes these roles are clear (the Concorde supersonic transport on the one hand, the innovations of Sony on the other), but they are often treated as the same thing. Let us also clarify that economic rationality is at once procedural and instrumental. It is procedural in that it sets the rules of the game in the service of the particular objectives of individuals and their cooperation for mutual interest. It is instrumental in that it combines technical means in view of economic

efficiency—that is, at the level of society, the greatest sum of utilities of individual consumers and, at the individual level, the maximization of one's own utility.

2. On the distinction between knowledge and practical knowledge, see Michael Oakeshott, *Rationalism in Politics* (Indianapolis: Liberty Fund, 1991), 12–17.

3. Quoted in Robert N. Bellah et al., *The Good Society* (New York: Knopf, 1991), 117. On the analysis of costs and benefits applied to human life, see pp. 115–19.

4. On the difference between working with wood and stone and working with iron, a "whore of a material," see the text full of profound insight by Péguy, *Deuxième Elégie XXX*, in *Oeuvres complètes en prose*, vol. 2, 942 f., and the commentary on it by Alain Finkielkraut in *Le Mécontemporain* (Paris: Gallimard, 1990), 53–61.

5. The environmental movement, born in reaction against techno-science, is not, it seems to me (despite undeniable virtues), up to the task of halting its progress where the substance of life is concerned. The main weakness of the environmental movement or rather movements is that of our age: an incoherent vision of man, stripped of his nature by equality by default. In its extreme version, environmentalism becomes explicit antihumanism (see Luc Ferry, *Le Nouvel Ordre écologique* [Paris: Grasset, 1992]). This antihumanism styles itself as revolutionary, but it is built on contemporary soil, that is to say, on the ruins of humanism. In this sense, it belongs to the world of late modernity.

CHAPTER 12

1. J. L. Missika, "La République des médias," *Pouvoirs*, no. 68 (1994): 107.

2. Here we leave aside issues relating to specifically political bias or disinformation. On this question, see especially Jean-François Revel, *La Connaissance inutile* (Paris: Grasset, 1988).

3. For a scholarly confirmation concerning what contemporary experience teaches, see John P. Robinson et al., *The Main Source: Learning*

from Television News (Beverly Hills: Sage Publications, 1986).

4. Alain Finkielkraut, *La Mémoire vaine* (Paris: Gallimard, 1989), 119.

5. Jacques Ellul, "L'Information aliénante," in *Propagandes* (Paris: Economica, 1990), 337.

6. Plato, *Republic,* bk. 4.

CHAPTER 13

1. Charles Taylor, *The Ethics of Authenticity* (Cambridge, Mass.: Harvard University Press, 1992). Nietzsche wrote, "[I]t is the peculiar *right of masters* to create values" (*Beyond Good and Evil,* 261).

2. Recall that we do not intend to imply that all sociologists, all nurses, and others cited in the examples behave in this way, but that such is the tendency of late modernity.

CHAPTER 14

1. "Man," Jean Hamburger points out, "is totally dependent upon the complex world of living and non-living beings that surrounds him. . . . Biologically, man in isolation has no meaning." ("Le miel et la ciguë," *Commentaire,* no. 60 [Winter 1992–93]: 959.)

2. Gabriel Marcel, *Du refus à l'invocation* (Paris: Gallimard, 1940), 161.

3. Taylor, *The Ethics of Authenticity,* 37. See also chapter 4 of Taylor's *Malaise of Modernity* (Concord, Ont.: Anansi, 1991).

CHAPTER 15

1. Here is a striking example of the incoherence of opinion "fabricated" by survey research:

> Are you for or against the establishment of a single European currency?
> For: 59%, Against: 32%, No answer: 9%.
> Would you vote "yes" or "no" for the Maastricht treaty?
> Yes: 44%, No: 56%
> (B.V.A., France [17–18 September 1993], in *Le Monde* [21 September 1993].)

In your view, would it be better for France to:

(a) Let the franc float in order to stimulate the economy? 42%

(b) maintain a strong franc in order to facilitate the establishment of the European Monetary Union? 39%

(SOFRES [15–16 September 1993], in *Le Figaro* [20 September 1993].)

Cited in *Commentaire*, no. 64 (Winter 1993–94): 738. Other examples can be found in Edward A. Kent, "Just How Accurate Are Public Opinion Polls?" *Human Events* (April 1987): 290–94.

2. The validity of responses varies notably according to whether the pressure of a received opinion is at play and to what degree. Responses dealing with racism or homosexuality are obviously more uncertain than those which deal with departures for vacations. See, among other examples of opinions not matching behavior, those given by P. Favre, "Du mode d'emploi des sondages électoraux," *Esprit*, no. 4 (April 1975): 538–39; and B. S. Mensh et al., "Underreporting of Substance Use . . . ," *Public Opinion Quarterly*, no. 52 (1988): 100–24. And let us mention a final example (the interpretation of which is more delicate): television networks, so fond of surveys, do not make programming decisions based on opinion surveys. They distinguish the reported demand from actual response to supply—and the data from the electronic monitoring device confirms that they are right and their surveys wrong. This gap can be explained in two ways: either those surveyed modify their responses in order to conform to received opinion, or they are divided between that to which they aspire and that to which they actually succumb. Both interpretations may hold part of the truth. The second illustrates another weakness of surveys: they proceed as if human beings were never divided within themselves.

CHAPTER 16

1. Elisabeth Noelle-Neumann, *The Spiral of Silence: Public Opinion— Our Social Skin* (Chicago: University of Chicago Press, 1984).

2. Bertrand de Jouvenel, *De la souveraineté* (Paris: Librairie de Médicis, 1955), 363.

3. Henri Bergson, *Cours*, vol. 1 (Paris: P.U.F., 1990), 306.

4. Let us add that the practice of science is subject to certain conditions—intellectual freedom, material means—that science does not control. In particular, politics matters. The economist who believes himself to be entrenched in his discipline needs political power in order to work in peace, and a liberal political environment to enjoy intellectual freedom. The sociologist or political scientist who disdains the importance of political regimes would not work in the same way in the shadow of the Gestapo or the KGB. The positivist jurist who criticizes liberal constitutionalism has this freedom to criticize thanks only to the practical success of the theory he criticizes.

5. Let us be precise in order to avoid all misunderstanding: what is targeted here is obviously not the mere fact of criticizing racism or violations of the rights of man (correctly understood). Is it necessary to recall, for example, that racism, insofar as it abolishes the singularity of the person and asserts essential differences among human groups, does violence to substantive equality and thus to man's very humanity? What is targeted is a critique that masks or effaces other moral questions and that sometimes or often (in the United States, in France, and elsewhere) takes an obsessive and errant form. The fact that racism is an unhealthy attitude does not imply that all forms of antiracism are healthy. It is not enough to be on the right side in order to act rightly. (We apparently have not learned from the fate of antifascism.)

6. Here again a qualification may be useful: there is of course no question of preaching indifference in the face of misery but rather of pointing up the double standard practiced (by and large) by the dominant discourse, a double standard challenged by true charity: "Love begins at home," Mother Theresa said. Regarding this humanitarian discourse (in its dominant version) and the ravages of "victimization" in the West, see Pascal Bruckner, *La Tentation de l'innocence* (Paris: Grasset, 1995), pts. 2 and 3.

7. François Brune, *Les Médias pensent comme moi!* (Paris: L'Harmattan, 1993), 41–42.

8. The present analysis of the "fabrication" of opinion is limited to pointing out a few leading themes; of course it passes over a number of nuances and variations. To our knowledge, the precise and detailed study of this area remains to be written, whether the question concerns France, the United States, Germany, or elsewhere. It would be wrong to expect scientistic sociology, which by and large belongs to the dominant form of thought, to illuminate this question by itself.

CHAPTER 17

1. Marcel, *Du refus à l'invocation*, 49. For a synthetic presentation of Marcel's analyses concerning the encounter, see Roger Troisfontaines, *De l'existence à l'être. La Philosophie de Gabriel Marcel,* vol. 2 (Louvain and Paris: Nauwelaerts, 1968), ch. 1.

2. More generally, the "Romanesque truth" dispels the romantic illusion of individual autonomy. See the penetrating analyses that René Girard devotes to Cervantes, Flaubert, Stendhal, Dostoyevsky, and Proust in *Mensonge romantique et vérité Romanesque* (Paris: Grasset, 1961).

3. This discussion in no way means that reasoning reason is out of place where moral questions are concerned, but only that its role is subordinate. More precisely, it means the following: (1) one never reasons except for lack of something better; (2) one never reasons except within the framework of first principles and an orientation of being that escapes reasoning reason. In this area, reasoning reason is appropriate for treating intermediate ends, for clarifying choices, for discussing means, for taking account of the infinite diversity of circumstances (which is no small thing), but it is powerless to determine the fundamental orientations on which everything finally depends.

4. See especially: R. Linton, "Universal Ethical Principles: An Anthropological View," in *Moral Principles of Action*, ed. Ruth Nanda Anshen (New York: Harper, 1952), 645–60; Pitirim Sorokin, *Social and Cultural Dynamics*, vol. 2 (New York: Bedminster Press, 1962),

chs. 13–15; C. S. Lewis, *The Abolition of Man* (1943) (Glasgow: Collins, 1982); James Q. Wilson, *The Moral Sense* (New York: Free Press, 1993); Maurice Cusson, *Le Contrôle social du crime* (Paris: P.U.F., 1983), 290–97; Jean Piaget, *Le Jugement moral chez l'enfant* (1932) (Paris: P.U.F., 1985).

5. This common core, according to James Q. Wilson, can be summarized in four fundamental dispositions: the instinct of sympathy, the sense of equity, the valuing of self-control, the sense of duty (*The Moral Sense*, pt. 1). As to the variations, these come into play in a number of domains including sexuality, drugs, and offenses having to do with opinions. They also concern the range of moral rules: here one can draw an opposition between moral codes intended for what might be called internal usage (applicable only within the group) and those understood as universal.

6. *De l'existence à l'être*, vol. 1, 114.

EPILOGUE 1

1. [Trans.] Charles Péguy, *Eve*, in *Oeuvres poétiques complètes* (Paris: Gallimard, 1957), 1114, 1111. The following translation is more literal than poetic:

> And it will not be these frail honeys
> who will adorn us the day of judging
> And it will not be their poor bundles
> that will equip us the day of trembling.
>
> And it will not be our learned little masters
> who will adorn us the day of judging
> And it will not be these lamentable beings
> who will equip us the day of trembling.
>
> And it will not be their illustrious works
> That will adorn us the day of wrath

And it will not be these ponies and these calves
The day of the last prize and of the last wages.

(. . .) And we will trust nothing but the prayer veils
Because Jesus is the one who wove them for us
And we will trust nothing but the sails of destitution
Because Jesus is the one who hoisted them for us.

EPILOGUE 2

1. Franz Oppenheimer, "Retour à Mayence," *Commentaire*, no. 65 (Spring 1994): 91.

INDEX